SOFTWARE
ENGINEERING:
METHODS AND
TECHNIQUES

software engineering: methods and techniques

This report was produced by the Information Structures Subgroup of the Dutch Database Club.
The Dutch Database Club is a working party of the Dutch Computer Association (NGI).
This English edition has been made possible through the support of the European Commission.

J. Blank
M.M.H. Drummen
H. Gersteling

T.G.M. Janssen
M.J. Krijger
W.D. Pelger

WILEY-INTERSCIENCE PUBLICATION

JOHN WILEY & SONS
NEW YORK - CHICHESTER - BRISBANE - TORONTO - SINGAPORE

Library of Congress Cataloging in Publication Data:

Main entry under title:

Software engineering--methods and techniques.

Translated and updated from the Dutch.
"This report was produced by the Information Structures Subgroup of the Dutch Database Club."
"Wiley-Interscience publication."
1. Electronic digital computers--Programming.
I. Blank, J. II. Dutch Database Club. Information Structures Subgroup.
QA76.6.S61717   1983   001.64'25   83-10261
ISBN 0-471-88503-7

ISBN 0-471-88503-7
Printed in The Netherlands
10 9 8 7 6 5 4 3 2 1

<u>Evaluation of methods and techniques for the analysis, design and implementation of information systems.</u>

Contents

6

<u>Prologue</u>

After a first edition of this study-report in Dutch the
report has been translated and updated. This has been made
possible through the support of the European Commission
and the help of Mr. Ray Goodsir of Database Consultants
Europe, who has assisted in producing a respectable
English version.

As co-ordinator, I would like to thank the members of the
study-group for their energy and enthusiasm.
And I will not forget to thank all who helped to type,
edit, re-edit and publish this book.

It is hoped that the reader will find it of practical use.

J. Blank

The Haque, Holland, 1983.

Chapter 1. Introduction

The use of methods and techniques for building information systems is widely under consideration nowadays. In 1978 when the Subgroup of the Dutch Database Club took on the evaluation of some ten methodologies, much had to be discussed and explored.
This book gives the means of evaluating these methodologies.

To make it possible to describe methodologies in a consistent way and thus to be able to compare them, the evaluation-matrix proposed by Thunnissen (12) has been adopted. The subgroup strongly supports the use of the definition of four aspects on which any methodology should be judged. These aspects are: the philosophy, the working procedure, the documentation method and the project management method.
Furthermore the analysis, design and implementation of information systems should be arranged, put into phases. A rather classic phase arrangement has been chosen, a subjective choice.
Chapter two deals with the evaluation-method in more detail.

In chapter three the book describes briefly ten methodologies and gives an idea about each methodology's aspects and phases, as shown graphically in the evaluation matrices. The matrix itself is described in detail in chapter four, whereas some conclusions and recommendations are laid out in chapter five.

To strive for consistency is quite a task with a group consisting of several members from different fields of experience and from different organisations. The group however, has learnt very much from this study, not least of all that a continuous dedication has been necessary to understand each other and each others frames of references.

Using the presented system of evaluation, the reader should be able to evaluate other methologies for the analysis, the design and the implementation of information systems for himself.

10

The subgroup consists of:

ir. J. Blank   - Ministry of the Interior,
                          The Hague

ir. M.M.H. Drummen   - ADP Center of Rotterdam
                          (GRC)
                          Rotterdam

H. Gerstelling,B.Sc.-   Centre for Information
                          processing (CVI), Dutch
                          railways
                          Utrecht

ing. T.G.M. Janssen   - Association of Dutch Health
                          Funds (VNZ)
                          Zeist

drs. M.J. Krijger   - Data Processing Division,
                          Waterboard (DIV)
                          Rijswijk

drs. W.D. Pelger   - Berenschot Informatica
                          Utrecht

CHAPTER 2   Analysis-synthesis

This chapter contains the paper "Informatie: structuur of doolhof? Aanzet tot vergelijking van methoden en technieken", published in Informatie, number 2, volume 21, February 1980 (the Dutch monthly computing journal, red.). This article (published in Dutch by the DBC/Info subgroup), analyses the problem of studying and evaluating methods and techniques in a consistent manner.

Information: Structure or Labyrinth?

An attempt to evaluate methods and techniques.

Finding the best methodology for the analysis, design and implementation of information systems, seems important to user departments, EDP departments, standards organisations, manufacturers and indeed to almost every conceivable group in the information processing industry. This chapter outlines the factors which are important in the practical application of any of the methods and techniques available. It describes processes and data using a diagram known as the "system bicycle" and introduces an evaluation method based on an "evaluation matrix".

2.1   Introduction

The methods and techniques available for systems analysis and design, for "change analysis" and problem analysis, for project selection and project management, are too numerous to mention, let alone to know in detail. All are praised by some people and condemned by others. In appendix 1 a list of more or less well known methods is given. For example, in the journal "Informatie", a number of methods have been described. See "methodologies for information-research and the system design: BISAD, HIPO and SDM" (1), the overview of Hartman (2). In the international information industry literature, one also finds many articles on this subject (12). The question to be asked about all the methods is whether or not they meet the need of all the possible categories of people who need to use them i.e. of management, users, information analysts, programmers, data base administrators, project managers, etc. Whilst the methods and techniques advocated within any one methodology may individually be of great use to specific users, there is often no logical connection which ties their parts into a coherent whole. From the user's point of view it is most important to have at one's disposal a consistent set of methods to handle all aspects of the system cycle i.e. to handle the aspects of system design, documentation and project management. The question is, however, whether any one methodology can handle all these aspects or whether one can identify a consistent set of methods which covers the different phases and aspects in the system cycle.

The following sections describe which aspects play a role in building and using information systems, which phases can be recognized in the system cycle and which facets are of importance in considering the relevant tools. The problems of evaluating these methods will also be considered. This should lead to a better understanding of the possibilities of such a set of methods.

2.2   Problem area

Most automation projects are, in practice, initiated by interested management. Projects are started in order to improve the efficiency or the effectiveness of the company operations. The benefits anticipated may be in the form of lower costs to the company or of an improvement in the quality of the services offered by the company.

Projects may also be initiated by company employees who are familiar with automation principles or EDP department procedures. These projects also aim at improving the efficiency of the company through application of EDP tools.

The initial definition of a project often consists of only a vague problem description. Before the real problem areas within a project are clearly defined, it is not clear which automation tools are best adapted to accomplish the project goals. This problem is aggravated by the fact that many companies use a range of EDP tools whose facilities often overlap. If these tools are not integrated, much time can be lost in learning or applying new standards, and in duplicating work already done.

Those methods and techniques that aim at a more integrated, structured and standardized working procedure for the development of information systems appear to have grown in number during the last few years.

To examine this problem area we consider the system bi-cycle, created during stimulating discussions with Jager. Figure 2.1 shows this system bi-cycle.

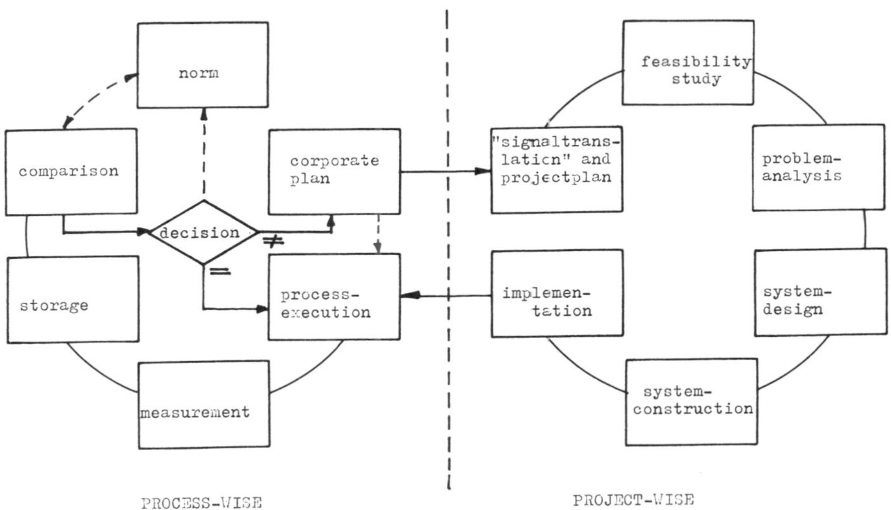

Figure 2.1: System-bicycle

The left hand cycle is the wheel which drives the system bicycle. It concerns the business processes which are essential to the successful functioning of the company. The execution of such corporate processes will normally be monitored, or measured, to see if the process in question accords with the overall company goals. The results of such checkpoint measurements will be stored and then compared against a set of predefined norms or standards. If there is no discrepancy, the process continues to play its role in the company's business cycle.

When the process results and the predefined norms are not in accordance with each other, the company goals outlined in the corporate plan must be consulted. A decision must then be taken as to whether or not the particular business process should be continued. In certain cases, the norms and standards must be changed.

The right hand wheel of the system bi-cycle shows the life cycle of one project. An individual project will be started in response to a signal from the business process cycle. The activities carried out within the project aim to produce a "product" which models the functioning of the business process concerned, or of the total information system of which the process is a part.

The phasing of activities within a project is a controversial subject. Two of the major problems that can occur with phases in a project are:

1. <u>Incompatible phase structures.</u>
   A phase structure which is ideal for systems design may group activities in a way which is inconvenient for any project management and control system.

2. <u>Level of detail.</u>
   The level of detail to which the analysis should be carried out often fluctuates wildly from phase to phase. In many cases the precise level of detailed analysis required is either vaguely defined or simply not defined at all.

Figure 2.1 attempts to show the different nature of the business process cycle on the left hand side, and the phases of the project development cycle on the right hand side. The operational

business processes are executed in a continuous loop, whereas project development is a single cycle loop which delivers a "product" into this continuous business cycle.
In this context, the terms "process" and "project" may be defined as follows:

Process: a grouping of company activities whose aim is to produce a definable output from a definable input. These activities may occur in sequence or in parallel. They may involve the actions of men as well as the handling of information. A characteristic of a process is that it can normally be repeated continuously, and that alternate methods may be developed to achieve the same goal.

Project: a grouping of activities, occurring in sequence or in parallel, whose aim is to produce an information "product" which will be incorporated into the company process structure. Characteristics of a project are:
    -it is executed once only.
    -it has a start date and an end date.
    -it has a predefined budget.
    -it serves one or more business processes.

The link between processes and projects is shown in the system bicycle diagram. This connection and the organisational implications are discussed in (4).

2.3   Analysis/synthesis

The project cycle starts with a "translation of signals" from the process loop. These signals are normally vague and often result from a series of operational bottlenecks. The initial project plan thus also tends to be vague.
It is a striking fact that the reasons for starting most projects are based on knowledge of the company which is carried in the heads of a few managers. Such knowledge rarely covers the needs of the company as a whole, and still more rarely is it written down, other than in a statement of general company goals. This means that many projects simply attack bottlenecks which are the

most obvious indication that something is wrong. The real cause of the problem, however, may go undetected and may simply create further bottlenecks at different points in the business loop.
This problem can be solved by creation of a medium term information processing plan. Such a plan should look at the total information processing needs of the company. This enables priorities to be arranged, and bottlenecks to be anticipated. The undertaking of any costly project can thus be done on a rational basis.
Projects which are ill-conceived rarely satisfy the user organisations which request them. Since automation costs are rising rapidly, users and EDP personnel alike want to have a set of tools which facilitate communication and allow for a great degree of control over project selection and development. This has resulted in a great deal of interest in methods and techniques which can be used to achieve these aims. Examples of such interest are illustrated by (5), (7).
In (7), reference is made to the importance of a strategic, or corporate, plan which is constructed by means of global corporate analysis and synthesis.
Such a plan can be seen as a "company model" i.e. a picture of a company's business operations showing all relevant processes, functions and information flows. Other associated techniques deal with the analysis of goals and with "value engineering" (3).
The building of such a "company model" is normally done by a team of people from the company itself, possibly assisted by specialist personnel. The first attempt at such a company analysis/synthesis should illustrate the company functions in global terms and the initial results should be presented to the executive management team for confirmation and discussion.
The level of detail of the analysis, and therefore the level of detail of the model produced , depends on the time and money one wishes to spend. The difficulty here is that no optimum level of detail can be given. Decisions on the direction of future information systems development can be hindered by too many details as well as by too few.
Much therefore depends on the experience and the expertise of the team selected to do the study.

Some typical problems that may be encountered in the study are:

a. <u>Process definition.</u>
It is often very difficult to define practical criteria for the identification of processes. Even when a candidate process is identified, it is often still more difficult to define the limits of that process and to agree on a standard method of process description.
There is a need for a method which describes processes and information in terms of a series of identifiable parameters. At this point in time, however, it is probably not feasible to attempt more than has been done in (8) and (9). Principles derived from mathematics and cybernetics may be of use here, and some rules based on the cybernetics of company processes are given in (11). The difficulty is to find an approach which is based on firm scientific principles, but which also leaves room for creative thinking on the part of the study team.
Once processes are defined, the company analysis/synthesis attempts to link them to entities (data classes, data streams etc.). This brings us to another problem area.

b. <u>Entity identification.</u>
There is no standard method of identifying and describing a conceptual entity. One must choose between a variety of methods which use terms such as: real entity, abstract entity, object, entity-attribute-relationship model. Opinions on which method is the best, vary enormously.

c. <u>Organisational units.</u>
The same type of problem is encountered in the attempt to relate processes to organisational units. Once again, it is difficult to define theoretical criteria for the definition of an organisational unit. This problem is compounded by the existence of informal organisational units such as commissions and work committees.

The problems outlined are typical of those which have to be dealt with when studying, evaluating or using any methods and techniques for the design of information systems.

Figure 2.2 shows the relation between the company analysis/ synthesis activities and the project selection to the detailed analysis and synthesis activities per problem area in the company model.

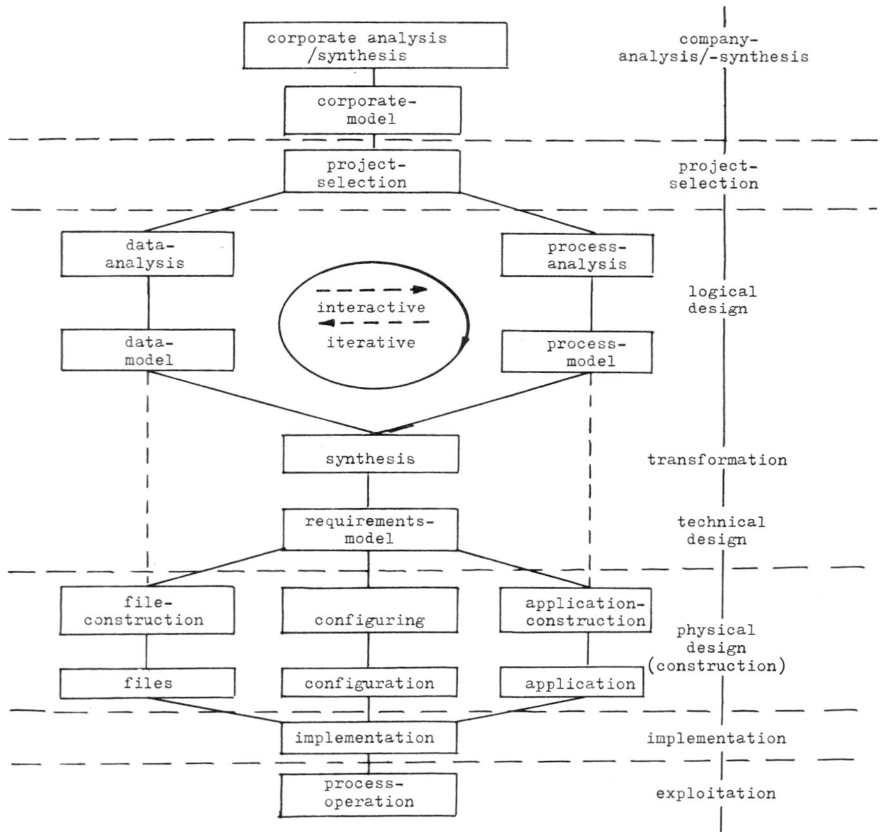

Figure 2.2: analysis/synthesis.

In general the methods that are "on the market" tend to group processes and entities into hierarchical structures. For example, processes are often grouped into a hierarchy of process, sub-process and elementary process. An elementary process can be seen as a grouping of activities that can't be subdivided in sub-processes. The elementary processes which occur within different divisions of a company are used as the basic building blocks of the process hierarchy. This has to do with the iterative character of process analysis/synthesis and with the levels of increasing and decreasing abstraction.

In practice the methods wich are used are based upon the process approach (grouping and description of processes), or upon the entity approach (grouping and description of entities through input-output analysis). The methods used in both approaches are based upon either a top-down approach or a bottom-up approach.
It is felt that neither a top-down nor a bottom-up approach is sufficient in itself. The project goals can be best achieved by using a combination of both approaches. A top-down, iterative approach should be used for process description and entity analysis, whereas a bottom-up, iterative approach should be used for synthesis (see figure 2.2).

2.4.   Project execution

After deciding on a strategic plan for the control of corporate processes in a particular problem area of the company, the execution of the selected project can start. Apart from the grouping of activities into phases, it is important to notice the differentiation between processes and entities. The duality between entities and activities (processes) is mentioned explicitly in (10). Apparently the same "four sided box notation" can be used to describe the activity diagrams as well as the entity diagrams.

The detailed analysis of processes deals with a description based upon the transformation of input data to output data, and the detailed entity analysis deals with the definition and description of data related to processes.

20

From a computer viewpoint, the first analysis
will lead finally to application programs and the
second to data structure design. The analysis
should be carried out interactively. Furthermore
it should be done in an iterative way, meaning
that a top-down detailed analysis should be
followed by a bottom-up synthesis to verify the
work already done. This bottom-up synthesis may
cause iteration if it uncovers errors in the
initial top-down analysis.

The process analysis will lead to a process model, consisting of a detailed description of the
processes considered from a computing viewpoint.
This detailed description shows connections
(information streams) between processes and also
shows if and where elementary processes occur in
the process grouping. This grouping may lead to
an optimisation of the application programs which
will eventually be written. For a consistent way
of describing activities, elementary processes
etc. a suitable language is needed (process
definition language, see 8, 9 and 10).

The entity analysis (data analysis) activity
results in an entity model (data model) and a
description of the relevant entities, properties,
attributes and relationships (structures). The
entities are related to elementary processes in
which they occur. This detailed description can
lead to "automaticaly produceable data storage
structures" with the aid of software generators.
For consistent description of data, properties,
attributes and relationships, a suitable language
is needed (data definition language). The Codasyl
proposals could possibly meet this need.

The final synthesis leads to the draft of a
"requirements-model". The draft describes the
"product" that has to be delivered by the intended project in order to achieve the desired
goals. A concrete estimate of the possibilities
and their costs is necessary at this moment. If
the decision to produce a specific product is
taken, the design, construction and the implementation phases will follow (see also figure 2.1).

After implementation, the target business process will be "enriched" by the addition of the
project "product". This may mean that the com-

pany's internal procedures are made more econo-
mical or efficient, or that the quality of service offered by the company is improved.

2.5. Approach to evaluation.

The process and data analyses have to be perfor-
med in a standard manner (see also $\underline{8}$) in order to
guarantee a consistent project procedure and to
supply the user and the project manager with a
tool to manage and control the project execution.
The terms process and data have been used explicitly here to emphasize the dynamic aspect on the
one side and the static aspect on the other.
In the literature, different terms are used e.g.
functional analysis, data-driven-analysis, out-
put-input-analysis, precedence analysis, object-
analysis, (one could think of a parallel subject-
analysis), system analysis etc. The differences
in terminology makes us believe that, in this
respect, no consensus on a final standard
terminology has been reached in the computing
community.

In 2.6.a. we mention four viewpoints from which
to examine the effectiveness of methodologies
which use information and data analysis, i.e.
- the basis of a methodology; the _philosophy_ or
  the way of thinking,
- the application or use of the methodology being studied; the _working procedure_,
- the _documentation method_ used,
- the _project management_ used.

These four aspects seem to be critical when considering the use of the process and data analysis
within the structure of a project. This division
into four aspects was used by the subgroup as the
starting point for the evaluation of some ten
methods and techniques.

2.6. Evaluation method

The preceding text describes globally the problems the subgroup was confronted with in trying to evaluate methods and techniques that are on the market. As stated before the four aspects: philosophy, working procedure, documentation method and project management method have been used as a guide-line for the subgroup in the classification of these methods and techniques. Furthermore, it is important in such a classification to consider which aspects are relevant to which project phases. It appears that we are far from agreeing on the definition of standard phases of a project. In global terms most of the project phase definitions appear to be similar. As soon as we consider the details of activities per phase, the contents of the documentation to be produced and the management aspects involved, important differences come to light. These differences are a consequence of both the way of thinking, or the philosophy behind each methodology, and the way in which this philosophy is translated into a practical working procedure.
The working group does not by any means claim to have completely avoided subjectivity in matching the four aspects in question to the project phases.
In order to minimise such subjectivity, it was agreed to fit the evaluation results for each methodology into an agreed "evaluation matrix". The axes used in this matrix are described below.

a. The horizontal axis.

The way of thinking, philosophy, is seen as an essential basis for the application of any method or technique. This philosophy has to clarify what lies behind that method or technique when it is applied in practice. This implies that practical explanations of the terms and definitions used within the methodology must be given (e.g. definitions of "process" and "data"). The methodology should also give guidelines as to how to recognise the units it defines as its essential building blocks. For example, this requires that a methodology gives a description of the criteria that must be fulfilled by any candidate process in order to be designated as a process within the context of the methodology concerned.

Furthermore, the methodology should define its own formal language in order to speak of things such as a "process definition language".

The working procedure describes the way in which the basic philosophy is used, to tackle a practical problem. Such an area could be, for example, the analysis of a company, the process and/-or data analysis, the system design, the programming or the implementation. Here the formal definition of the terms used in each method are essential because they are the basic tools used in applying the theories in practice. If a top-down approach is advocated, the levels of abstraction have to be described in a quantitative as well as in a qualitative way. The way in which these levels are identified must also be defined. Different disciplines, which are needed to apply the theory in practice should also be mentioned and described.

The documentation method has to describe the documentation to be produced at each stage in the methodology. The contents of each document must be fully described. The description of how the documentation is to be produced is also very important (e.g. schema techniques, forms, guidelines for textual description). The organization of the documentation has to be described as well e.g. central/decentral documentation management, tools, documentation, classification, coding systems, retrieval methods etc. Mention must also be made of the person(s) for whom the document is produced.
Ideally, documentation concerning processes and data is gathered during the execution of the relevant methodology activities. The documentation produced must be integrated with the proposed project management procedures.

The project management method is a description of the way in which the project is to be structured to meet the defined goals. This description should include guidelines for project organisation, for the description of phases, activities, milestones, responsabilities, project interfaces, budgetary provisions, etc. Planning techniques and cost benefit analysis techniques must also be described.
It is crucial that the project management method

be applicable at any stage in the systems development cycle. The method must contain a "signal translation" mechanism which translates signals received from the business process cycle into a project plan. Conversely, it must contain a mechanism which allows the project "product" to be incorporated into the business process cycle. Any project management method must also be tuned to the philosophy, the working procedure and the documentation method of the host methodology. These four aspects form the horizontal axis of the evaluation matrix.

b. The vertical axis

The subgroup did not immediately agree upon the classifications within the vertical axis of the evaluation matrix. Vertical axis classification vary from methodology to methodology. A classification may be perfectly suitable for one methodology, but not when comparing it with other methodologies. The problem is then how to compare methodologies on this vertical axis.

For the present the subgroup has chosen the following classifications:

<u>company analysis/ -synthesis</u>	- process analysis, function oriented analysis - data oriented analysis - company information plan
<u>project selection</u>	- selection on the basis of priorities and of alternative solutions to bottlenecks
<u>logical design</u>	- detailed process analysis --> logical system design - detailed data analysis --> data structure design
<u>transformation</u>	- logical system design --> technical system design - data structure --> storage structure
<u>technical design</u>	- technical system design - technical file design

<u>physical design,</u> <u>construction</u>	- programming - description user procedures - description procedures of computercentre - file construction
<u>implementation</u>	- implementation of the system designed (including tests and conversion)
<u>operation</u>	- operation of the system implemented (including maintenance and tuning).

The divisions described above are used as the two axes of the evaluation matrix. This matrix is used to gain an insight into possible connections and overlaps between the methodologies studied.

In order to classify the methodologies, each member of the group described one or more methodologies using the classification system described above. Each description was discussed by the whole group.

Because of the time available those methods and techniques that deal explicitly with project management were excluded.

2.7. Structure in the labyrinth ?

This report emphasizes the importance of integrating automation products into the business processes of an organization. If this integration is to be successful, everyone in the company, from management level to operational level, must have a thorough understanding of the role of the methods and techniques used by DP personnel. The DP people, for their part, should attempt to become very familiar with the business processes of the company. This creates a mutual understanding which smooths the way for the acceptance of new automation products and leads to a better knowledge of the whole business process-to-project relationship.

This report does not attempt to deal with the organisational aspects of business processes or information projects. It would be possible to devote several chapters alone to this topic (<u>4</u>). The aim of the study is to evaluate some tools which can be used to find a structured path through the "information labyrinth" (see <u>5</u>, <u>6</u>). It should also be emphasised that there is not one such path which is ideal for every conceivable project and that there are many different possible approaches towards this information labyrinth.

References

(1) Bruijns   Methodologieen voor informa-
                     tie-onderzoek en het systeem-
                     ontwerp: BISAD, HIPO en SDM
                     Informatie, jaargang 20, nr.2
                     Amsterdam, Feb. 1978

(2) Hartman, W.   Ardi revisited of het ontwer-
                     pen van informatiesystemen
                     Informatie, jaargang 21, nr.2
                     Amsterdam, Feb. 1978

(3) Forrester,J.W.   Industrial Dynamics
                     Cambridge (Mass.), M.I.T.,
                     Jonh Wiley & Sons, 1961,pp463

(4) Wedekind,H.   Systemanalyse
                     Carl Hanser Verlag
                     Munchen 1973

(5) Zanten, J.H.v.   Het vaststellen van een stra-
                     tegie voor geautomatiseerde
                     gegevensverwerking
                     Het Financieel Dagblad, 13 en
                     24 maart 1979

(6) Greve,W.B.de   Ziekenhuismarketing en stra-
                     tegische beleidsvoering
                     Het Ziekenhuis, 9e jaargang,
                     nr.5, 7 maart 1979

(7) Wissema,J.G.   Aanpassing beleidsplannen en
                     doelstellingen aa veranderde
                     organisatiestructuur
                     Het Financieel Dagblad, 3 en
                     7 april 1979

(8) Wedekind,H.   On the parametric specifica-
                     tion of database oriented in-
                     formation systems
                     Datametrics, Vol.5 (1976),
                     nr. 5

(9) Wang,C.P.   Parametrization of Informa-
                     tion Systems applications
                     IBM-Research Laboratory, San
                     Jose, California, April 11,
                     1973, Computer Sciences

(10) Ross,O.T.   Structured Analysis (SA): A
                         language   for   communicating
                         Ideas
                         IEEE Transactions on Software
                         Engineering, Vol.SE-3, no.1,
                         Jan. 1977

(11) Peters, L.J.   Comparing software design me-
      Tripp,L.L.   thodologies
                         Datamation, November 1977,
                         pp.89-94

Appendix 2.1

List of methods and techniques.

1. SADT (Softech, UK): Structured Analysis and Design Technique.

2. ISAC (RIT-Stockholm): Information Systems work and Analysis of Change research group.

3. BSP (IBM, USA): Business System Planning.

4. MOS (Desisco, the Netherlands): Modulair Ontwikkelen van Systemen.

5. SASO (IBM, the Netherlands): Systeem Analyse, Systeem Ontwerp.

6. NIAM (CDC, Europe)

7. PSL-PSA (Teichrow, USA): Problem Statement Language- Problem Statement Analyzer.

8. PDS (VRO/BiZa, the Netherlands): Project Documentatie- en ontwikkelingssysteem.

9. Bubble Charting (Martin): Analysis method Martin, Codd, Date.

10. SDM (Pandata, the Netherlands): System Development Methodology.

11. PROMPT (SYMPACT, UK): Project Resource Operation Management & Planning Technique.

12. PARAET (RAET, the Netherlands): Project Aanpak Methodiek.

13. GOS (CAP, the Netherlands): Gestructureerd Ontwerpen van Systemen.

14. Jackson method (USA).

15. Constantine-method (USA).

16. Warnier/Orr-method (France).

17. Nassi/Shneidermann-method.

18. PRODOSTA (Philips, the Netherlands): Project
    Documentatie Standaard.

19.   TNDS   (Thissen,   F.R.Germany):   Thissen
    Niederrheinisches Dokumentations System.

20.   PERT: Program Evaluation and Review
    Technique.

21. HIPO (IBM, USA): Hierarchy plus Input,
    Process, Output.

22. BISAD (HB, USA): Business Information Systems
    Analysis and Design.

23. MADDS (SIF, Norway): Methods and Aids for
    Development of DB-oriented Systems.

24. SMX (CGN, the Netherlands): Systematrix.

Chapter 3. Description per method.

In this chapter, each of the ten methodologies studied is described in terms of its philosophy, working procedure, documentation method and project management method. The completed evaluation matrix is discussed, and each subchapter terminates with a series of general observations.

Each methodology is discussed under the following headings:
1. Outline of the methodology
   - Philosophy
   - Working procedure
   - Documentation method
     - technique
     - organisation
     - contents
   - Projectmanagement method

2. Evaluation matrix

3. Applicability of the methodology
   - Description of the matrix coverage
   - Thoroughness of the methodology
   - Row transition
   - Column transition

4. Observations

The results of the overall evaluation matrix classification are described in chapter 4, and final conclusions and recommendations are presented in chapter 5.
In appendix 1 some references are given.
The different terms used in each methodology are compared in appendix 3. Appendix 2 defines the frame of reference for appendix 3.

3.1. BSP

This subchapter has been updated to reflect the later versions of BSP. The first edition of this study only considered the first version of BSP.

.1.   Outline of the methodology

.1.1. Philosophy

The Business Systems Planning (BSP) methodology attempts to apply a structured approach to the development of an "information systems plan" for a company or an organisation. Such a plan should help to meet the company's short term and long term information handling needs. It must also be integrated with the objectives of the company plan ("corporate plan" in BSP). This means that the "information systems plan" must reflect the viewpoint of the company top management. In order to achieve this, top management must take an active part in the BSP study.

The basis of the BSP-philosophy is the idea of the <u>process</u>. The company (business in BSP) <u>processes</u> are the essential activities and decisions that allow for the control and the administration of the operations (activities and services for achieving company goals) and the resources (financial, personnel and materials) of a company/organisation.

According to BSP, identification of the company processes achieves the following:
- it furthers a thorough understanding of the way in which a company pursues its goals
- it provides a tool for the identification of organisational responsibilities
- it forms a basis for a better insight into information needs
- it provides the means to distinguish between management control processes and operations processes.

BSP expects to identify about four to twelve main processes (process groups) in a company. Each of these processes can be subdivided into a number of other processes. The total number of such subdivisions can vary from twenty to sixty.

In the description of BSP in the "Information Systems Planning Guide" (<u>2</u>) examples of processes for eight business types are documented.

Although there is no clear "formula" for defining the processes, the methodology states that they are "defined as groups of logically related decisions and activities required to manage the resources of the business". The approach is to relate <u>processes</u> to:
- the <u>resources</u>, according to the four-stage life cycle of a product/service (requirements, acquisition, stewardships, retirement)
- the <u>data classes</u>, which are the basic units to be found in the company information streams. Normally from 30 to 60 such classes can be identified.
- the <u>organisational units</u>, involved in the execution of processes
- the <u>information systems</u>, which support the organisation units and are part of the information systems plan.

In this respect, a data class is a "category of logically related information", where these categories can be seen as "(<u>business</u>) entities" usually including, but not restricted to, the resources around which the (business) processes are defined.

In the BSP approach, the information architecture is constructed via the identification, and subsequent composition, of these processes, data classes and organisational units. Critical to the BSP methodology, however, is the idea that the "top-down analysis" used to build the information architecture is followed by a "bottom-up implementation."
A BSP-study of a company leads to a description of the functioning of that company where processes, data-classes, organisation units and information systems are mutually related. This description is management oriented in such a way that management can easily decide upon proposed alternate solutions and upon the proposed information systems planning, including systems priorities.
An alternate approach to the BSP-application is to start with a basic model for a company. The basic processes in this model may be expanded to

some twenty to sixty to reflect the actual company.
This is provided by the <u>generic process model</u> (<u>6</u>) of figure 3.1.1 where:

-Demand   : "translation" of the demand for a product/service from customers
-Supply   : "translation" of the supply of resources into a product/service
-Requirements   : determining and defining the requirements to correlate demand and supply, under influence of rules, prescriptions and regulations from the 'environment' (marketplace, governments etc.)
-Administration: control of, accounting for and registration of all practical tasks between demand and supply.
-Management   : planning, control and measurement of these four mutually dependent processes.

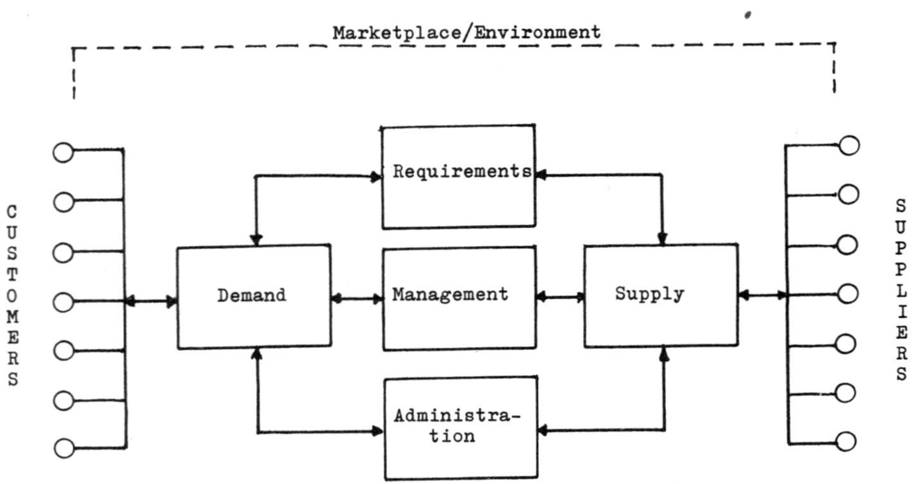

Figure 3.1.1.
    <u>Business process matrix/generic process model.</u>

One final factor of importance in the BSP philosophy is the idea of the <u>information life cycle</u>
shown in figure 3.1.2.

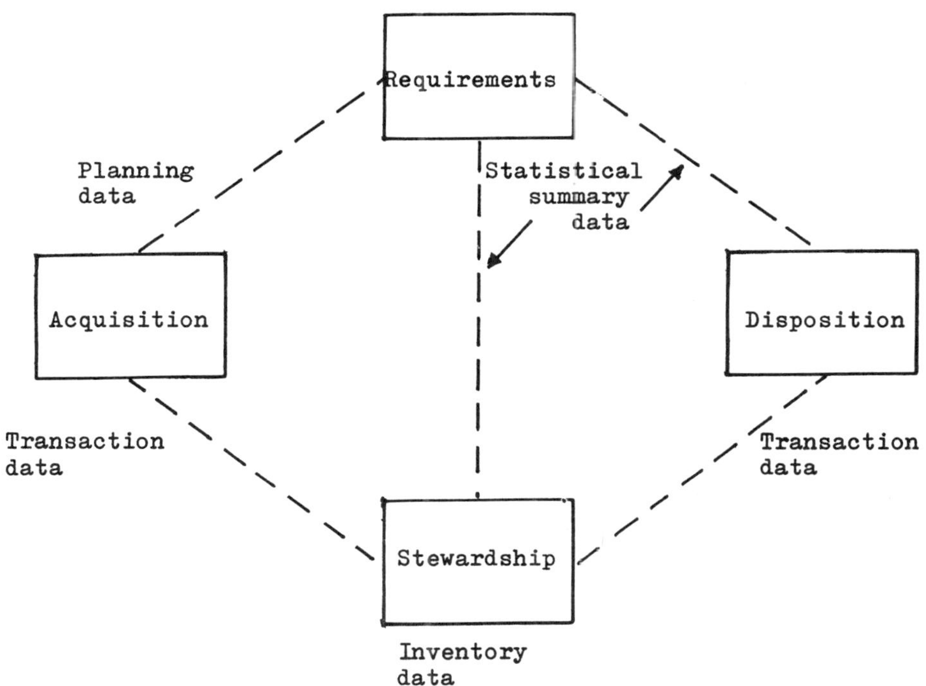

<u>Figure 3.1.2: Information life cycle</u>

In this information life cycle, the data and processes are related as follows:
- Planning data (objectives, expectations),which
  support requirement activities
- Inventory data (resource status), which support stewardship activities
- Transaction data, which cause changes in inventory by acquisition or disposition
- Summary data (periodic) from inventory,
  provide feedback.

.1.2 Working procedure

As previously stated, the BSP working procedure is based on the concept of top-down analysis and a bottum-up implementation. The left-hand side of figure 3.1.3 shows the steps in top-down analysis and the right-hand side shows the steps in bottom-up implementation.

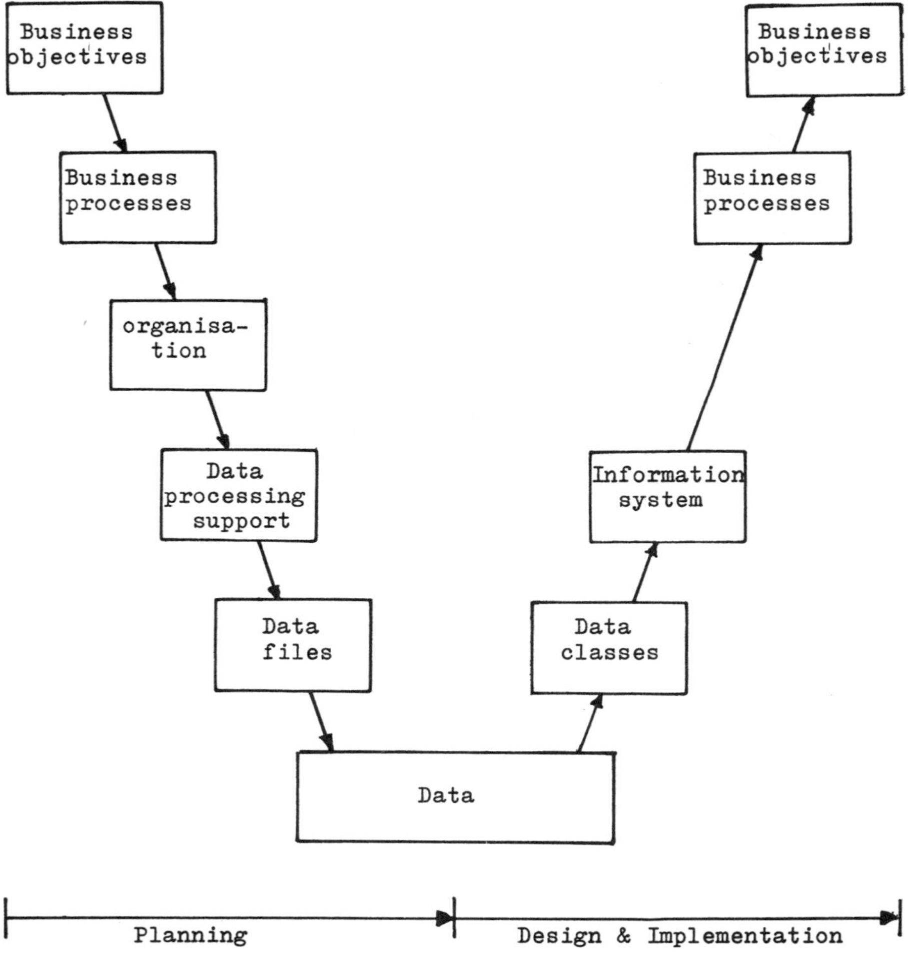

Fig.3.1.3. BSP top-down analysis
and bottum-up implementation.

There are eleven activities to be undertaken in the BSP study itself. Prior to commencing these activities, however, two other activities are essential. These are:
      1. To gain the support of a top executive

> sponsor and to ensure the involvement
> of this sponsor and other executives in
> the study.
> 2. To educate all people who may be invol-
> ved in the study by informing them the
> BSP objectives and working procedures.

The eleven actual study activities are summarised below.

1.2.1. Starting the study

After a preparation period of two weeks, the study team conducts a "kick-off" meeting to review its own workplan. The total BSP study should take approximately six weeks. At this meeting, the company goals are reviewed as are the information systems now operational or under development.

1.2.2. Defining business processes

The company processes are now defined according to the four-stage life cycle of products/-services. The processes are identified, flow-charted, decomposed and grouped, fully described and then related to organisational units. Finally, potential key processes are identified and their importance is checked by interviewing the people concerned. As far as possible, these processes should be identified independently of the current company structure.

The major output of this activity is a list of processes and their description. The organisation/process matrix relates processes, or groups of processes, to the people or organisational units concerned. It also shows whether or not a person or organisational unit has major responsability for a process. Influence on the process concerned is determined to be in one of three categories:
- major decision-making responsibility
- major involvement
- some involvement

Examples of processes are given in the appendices of BSP (6). Here the "generic process model" can be very helpful.
BSP recognises some ten main processes with 20 to 60 processes in total.

1.2.3.   Defining data classes

To define the data classes two approaches are suggested:
1. The business entity approach, where the four types of data classes mentioned under philosophy (page 35) are related to business entities in a matrix. "Entities are things an organisation is concerned about such as customers, products, materials, personnel etc.".
2. The business process approach, where "input-process-output" diagrams are constructed to identify data classes used or created by each process.

The results of 1.2.2 and 1.2.3 are combined and lead to the construction of a process/data class matrix which shows creation (C) and usage (U) of data for each process. Some 30 to 60 data classes are thus identified

1.2.4.   Analysing current systems support

Using the results obtained so far, the BSP team can now determine:
- which processes are not supported via executing systems.
- which processes are supported in some organisational units but not in others.
- which systems are redundant.

BSP shows how to register these results in a system/organisation matrix and a system/process matrix. These techniques should also be applied to the usage of data by existing systems. This leads to the system/data-class matrix which shows whether existing systems relate to data on existing files.

1.2.5.   Determining the executive perspective

In this activity the list of executives to be interviewed ("no more than two levels below the president") is confirmed, an interview schedule is drawn up, and the interview questions are prepared.
The actual interviews are conducted using wall charts which outline topics such as: 'objectives of the study', 'scope of the study', 'organisa-

itself and assisted by an IBM representative. The characteristics of team members is mentioned in tion', 'system/organisation matrix', etc.
The results of the interviews are documented and used as input to the next step.

1.2.6.   Defining findings and conclusions

The interview results are reviewed in order to identify problems, solutions, value statements, processes impacted and processes causing problems.
This outcome can be summarised in an 'interview analysis and data reduction sheet'.

The interview data are classified in three categories:
-   IS problems/solutions and values (existing system)
-   IS needs and values (non existing systems)
-   non-IS problems.

The last category is not handled within the BSP methodology. However the information gathered in the interviews may well be of use in formulating solutions for non-IS problems.

The results of this activity are summarised in a problem/process matrix which provides a valuable basis for making further recommendations, for designing the information architecture and for assigning systems priorities.

1.2.7.   Defining information architecture

To define the information architecture, the BSP study-team determines how the data should be managed to support the processes. The data classes defined are logically grouped into databases.
An information-architecture is defined using the basic diagram of figure 3.1.4.
The diagram is used as a blueprint for systems design in each business area. For each area it shows:
        -   the data to be created, controlled and used
        -   the relationships between each system to be built.
        -   the systems which support a given business process.

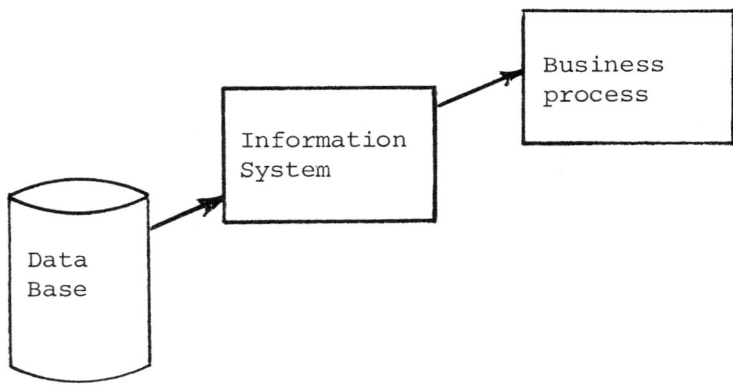

<u>Fig.3.1.4.</u> Relationship of data to systems and the processes supported.

The process/data-class matrix of activities 1.2.2 and 1.2.3 is manipulated in such a way as to group processes and data into major system areas. Data classes which are used in one systems area and created in another are used to establish the basic information flow between systems (see figure 3.1.5 or refer to the BSP documentation for a more complete example).
The systems areas are given names like 'manage-ment', 'requirements', 'manufactoring', 'sales', 'administration' and 'personnel', according to the thus grouped processes and data classes involved.
The information architecture can thus be built in a series of structured steps.
The final graphic rearrangement of this architec-ture has all the resemblances with the 'generic process model' (figure 3.1.1)

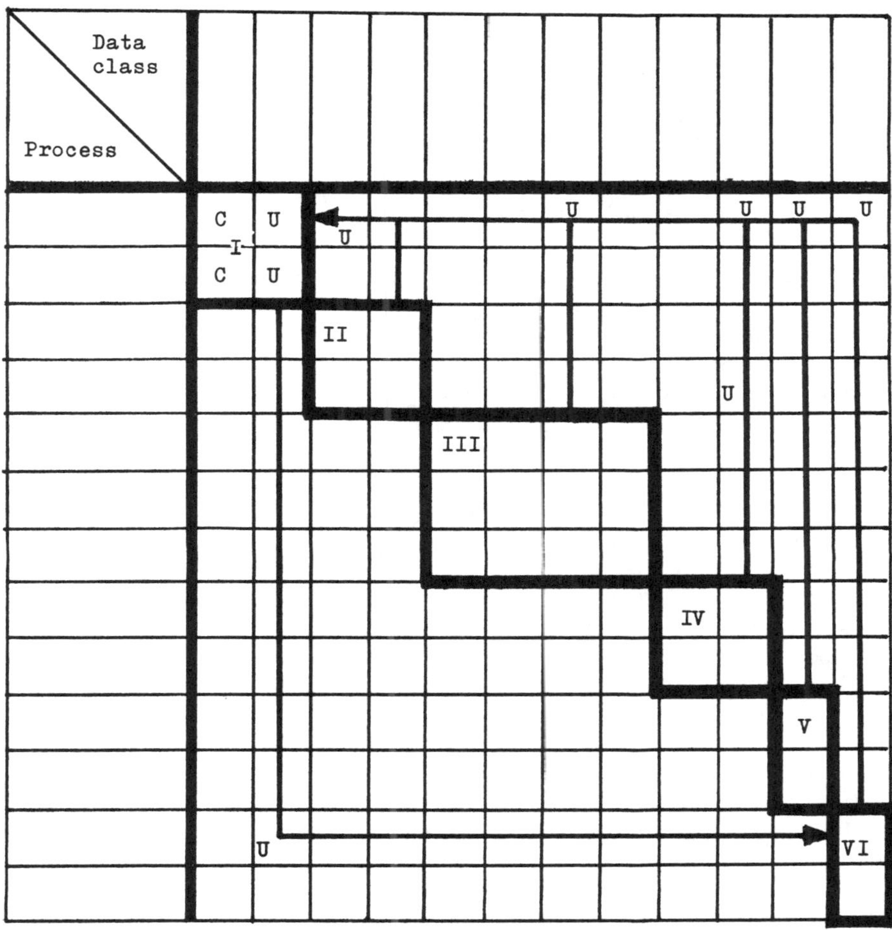

Figure 3.1.5. The process/data-class matrix.

BSP says that the _identification of subsystems_ is an arbitrary classification. However, a working procedure is given where each C (see activity 1.2.3) is defined as a _create subsystem_ and each U defined as a _usage subsystem_. Logical combinations and/or splits can be made.

When the subsystems are defined a description of
the functions within each is documented.
Using the resulting information architecture, the
interdependencies between subsystems can be analysed, and the results shown in a prerequisite
subsystem analysis matrix, indicating which
subsystem should be available before others can
be constructed.

1.2.8.   Determining architecture priorities

Whereas the information architecture provides a
blueprint showing the place of each system and
the relationships between systems, this activity
aims at determining the architecture priorities.
This means that each step to be taken in the
"development" of the information systems must be
determined.
The criteria to be used are grouped into four
categories:
- potential benefits (tangibles, intangibles, return on investment)
- impact (organisational, people, quality etc.)
- success (acceptance, probability of implementation, resources)
- demand (value of existing systems, relationship
  to other systems, needs).

Finally, a recommendation is made as to which system (or subsystem) should be implemented first.
This system must be documented in sufficient
detail to allow the executive(s) concerned to
make a proper evaluation of the proposals.
These proposals should be accompanied by a
risk-benefit-analysis which focuses on the
financial justification of the project. The costs
should also be itemised according to the priorities which have been determined.

1.2.9.   Reviewing information-resource management

This activity reviews the Information Resource
Management (IRM) in order to recommend immediate
changes and to specify IRM activities necessary
to implement the proposed information-architecture.
This analysis and the recommendations should be
aimed at the IR management levels and should not
deal with all the detailed IRM functions.
The purpose of IRM is "to manage IS resources for

the most efficient and effective support of the
business" and to provide for "the continuous
planning, control, measurement and operation of
the information".

This BSP study activity should result in the
following IRM outputs:
- findings and conclusions concerning general
  aspects of IRM
- IR objectives
- definition of the high-priority IRM projects
- recommendations for immediate actions
- a plan of action for follow-on projects.

1.2.10. Developing recommendations and an action
         plan.

BSP study recommendations focus on:
- information architecture
   .detailing the subsystems present in the
    overall information network
   .interim improvements to current systems.
- information systems management
   .data administration for the control of the
    organisation's data resources
   .information-systems planning to ensure an
    information-architecture which is responsive
    to changing conditions
   .measurement and control of actual and future
    implementations.
   .distributed information systems in order to
    determine possibilities for the distribution
    of hardware, data and processes and software
    development.
- architecture priorities
   .development plans for the high priority sy-
    stems to be implemented.

If a project is specified for the implementation
of any of the recommendations, it should be
accompanied by an action plan.

1.2.11. Reporting results

The final activity concerns the preparation of
the study report and the presentation of the
study results to executive management.
A report outline is prepared, the report is written and the presentation medium is determined.
The executive presentation is then prepared and

delivered.

The BSP-study ends with the development of an action plan for the follow-on activities and the presentation of this plan for management approval. The BSP-Guide gives an overview of possible follow-on activities.

Perhaps the most important BSP follow-on activity is the determination of which person or group of persons is responsible for continuing the process of IS planning.
The study results can thus be used as a basis for a consistently maintained long-range IS plan.

Another important follow-on activity is, of course, the implementation of the first system as recommended by the study plans.

.1.3. Documentation method

Much of the BSP documentation is produced during the execution of the above activities. This sub-chapter considers the documentation produced from three points of view, i.e. content, organisation and techniques.

.1.3.1 Content:

Pre-BSP phase: Gaining the commitment and Preparing for the study.
- brief 'factors report' on reasons for BSP study   : headings
- study announcement letter to executives
                                : example
- study work plan
                                : example
- BSP study control file
                                : suggested contents

N.B. This control file is important because of the number and nature of the documents involved in the study.

- outline and table of contents of study report
                                : content per capita
- executive interview list + schedule + topics.
- interview confirmation letter
                                : example.

1. Starting the study
   - information about the business goals, objectives and strategies etc. Selected documentation (material) or hard copies for use in the study.   : presentation
   - summary on information systems support; idem   : presentation

2. Defining business processes:
   - notes concerning definitions of processes and important decisions within processes
   - description of product and resources flow diagram   : pre BSP
   - examples of process groups and processes by industry   : BSP-appendix
   - examples of planning and control processes   : BSP-appendix
   - general flowchart of the product/service processes   : example
   - description of each process (notes)
   - short description or list of resource components
   - organisation/process matrix   : example

3. Data classes
   - data class/business entity matrix   : example
   - input-process-output diagrams   : example
   - data class/process matrix   : example

4. Business/systems relationships
   - system/data-file matrix   : example
   - organisation/process matrix   : example
   - system/organisation matrix   : example
   - system/process matrix   : example
   - examples of matrices from other industries   : BSP-appendix

5. Executive perspective
   - executive interview list + schedule + topics and questions

- interview reports (notes) and summaries
- wall charts (with matrices etc.), sample
  list   : BSP-appendix

6. Business problems
   - worksheet for interview analysis and data
     reduction   : example
   - interview notes + addendum(s)
   - flipchart page for each process group and
     its processes
   - problem/process matrix

                                    : example

7. Information architecture
   - several iterations of a process/data class
     matrix   : examples
   - data flow determination matrix/diagram

                                    : example
   - data flow diagram

                                    : example
   - information architecture

                                    : example
   - graphic rearrangement

                                    : example
   -   identification   and   description   of
     subsystems
   - prerequisite subsystem analysis matrix
                                    : example

8. Priorities
   - sample subsystem ranking

                                    : example
   - list of steps or projects necessary for im-
     plementation of the first system
   - documentation of recommended systems
                                    : cf.company standard
   - subsystem/risk level matrix, example
                                    : BSP-appendix

9. IRM
   - IRM processes, example

                                    : BSP-appendix
   - flow of IRM activities

                                    : example
   - list for IRM development priorities
   - IS objectives description, changes
                                    : example
   - list of IRM changes to support architectural
     priorities
   - categorisation of problems and required IRM

        changes
        - categorisation of problems by IR-process

10.Recommendations
    - description of recommendations
    - description of action plans (projects)

11.Report
    - report outline
    - report of BSP-study results
    - executive presentation and summary
                        : content per chapter

.1.3.2   Organisation

No suggestions are given for the organisation of
the documentation. BSP states that all the
documents should be stored in the Study Control
File and that this file should be available to
all members of the study team. Secretariat
support is an important factor in a BSP study.

.1.3.3   Techniques

In addition to the normal technique of textual
descriptions, BSP uses a number of matrices to
show the relationships between processes, data,
organisational units and systems. It also favours
the use of input-process-output diagnosis. For
discussions, it suggests the use of wall charts.
All documentation is manual as opposed to being
computer-produced. In the latest BSP version, the
use of a Data Dictionary facility is introduced.

.1.4   Project management method

The BSP methodology does not contain a fully
developed project management method as such. It
does recommend that, before a BSP study is
started, a work plan and an associated time plan
should be prepared. This plan should cover an
approximate elapsed period of from 8 to 10 weeks.
The BSP study itself takes from 6 to 8 weeks, but
2 weeks are required for preparation.

The study is carried out by a team, chaired by a
team leader (co-ordinator) from the company

itself and assisted by an IBM representative. The characteristics of team members is mentioned in the BSP-guide.
A study team organisation, which includes recommendations on the role of the team secretary and the IBM-representatives, is suggested.
The study activities are all executed in sequence, apart from reviewing "information systems management, 9" which is carried out in parallel with "defining information architecture, 7" and "priorities, 8". Control points are given as well as recommendations as to who should do the controlling or be involved in it.

.2. <u>Evaluation-matrix BSP.</u>

		philosophy	working procedure	documentation method			project-management method
				tech	org	cont	
Company analysis/ synthesis	1.1						
	1.2						
	1.3						
project-selection							
Logical design	3.1						
	3.2						
Logical → technical	4.1						
	4.2						
Technical design	5.1						
	5.2						
Physical design	6.1						
	6.2						
	6.3						
	6.4						
implemen-tation							
exploita-tion							

.3. Applicability of the methodology.

BSP should be used primarily to provide top management with an insight into how information systems might support company goals. The aim of a BSP study is to produce a Business (Information) Systems Plan which will provide guidelines for subsequent projects. These guidelines for further action should be in accordance with the business priorities of the company.

.3.1 Description of the matrix coverage.

The BSP-methodology seems to aim at covering the upper two rows of the evaluation matrix: the company analysis/ synthesis and the project selection.
The basic idea is to define a company/ organisation in terms of its business processes. These processes should be defined independently from the current company structure. Once they are defined, they are related to organisational units, data classes and information systems.
The terms used in this approach are not defined precisely, but illustrative examples are given to clarify their meaning. Some further classifications may be found in the BSP glossary.
Much however remains to be defined, classified and categorised by the study team. The working procedure of the methodology is therefore aimed at this study team, which is supplied with guidelines (checklists, examples, content descriptions etc.). A capable team leader and top management support are important to the successful implementation of the BSP guidelines.

The methodology does not clearly define a means of identifying processes or data classes. Organisational units and information systems are more easily identified, although they are also reviewed in the kickoff meeting.

BSP is not supported by a full documentation method, although it does say what should be documented. It does not specify in full detail the form of documentation. Furthermore, no appropriate tools other than the IBM DB/DC data dictionary facility (rel. 3) to use for documentation development are mentioned. It does not say how

this is to be achieved.
The project management method given is restricted to the 8 to 10 weeks of the BSP-study. In the chapter on the follow-on activities, project organisation and management are mentioned, but no strict rules are given. BSP wants to conform to company standards, which seems to be practical in so far as IRM is concerned. Further project stages are outside the scope of BSP. However, phased development is suggested and a reference is made to "Managing the Application Development Process" (6).

.3.2 Thoroughness of the methodology.

Because there is room for considerable scope in the interpretation of BSP terms and definitions, the study team must have a thorough understanding of company procedures in order to be successful.

BSP does not attempt do deal with the later stages of project development. It confines itself to the definition of processes and sub-processes. No attempt is made to define the elementary processes and activities as defined in appendix 2.

Data is defined in terms of "classes". But the definition of what constitutes different levels of data classes is left to the study team. The same is true for subdivisions of organisational units and information systems.

The documentation descriptions are rather extensive throughout the BSP-methodology and should lead to a good description of the company's information system problems and recommended solutions.

.3.3 Row transition.

The BSP-methodology covers the first two rows of the evaluation matrix company analysis/synthesis and project selection.
Within the analysis/synthesis BSP gives an overall analysis/ synthesis of processes leading to a process-structure and links this in a natural way to the overall analysis/synthesis of data with the grouping into data-classes.

In the <u>analysis/synthesis</u> row, BSP provides adequate tools for the understanding and documentation of the process structure within a company. It provides tools for the definition of data structures, in terms of data classes, and for linking these data structures to the relevant processes. BSP does not address the problem of building a comprehensive company data structure.

The units of the proposed information architecture diagrams can be rearranged to provide a company (information) model which shows the relationships between processes, data classes, organisational units and information systems. An organized approach to project selection can be derived from the IRM review, the priorities ascertained and the recommendations for developments.
The connection between the activities to be carried out in these two rows (or stages) and the interface to an IRM strategy are two of the strongest points of the BSP methodology.
The connection with further stages (logical design etc.) is outside the scope of BSP, although an overview of follow-on activities is given in the guide.
Standardised documentation techniques such as HIPO and structured walk-throughs are mentioned as aids to the efficiency of system implementation. Further possible connections to other methodologies which may be of use in the follow-on project stages have not been explained.

.3.4 Column coordination.

It is impossible to separate the BSP philosophy from its working procedures. The philosophy is not presented as a separate subject but is instead integrated with the tasks of the working procedures presented to the user as a series of ideas interspersed amongst the practical tasks of the working procedures.

The ideas behind the steps in the working procedure seem to be sound and the procedures themselves also seem practical. The documents used throughout the working procedure serve as the basic units for the complete BSP documentation.

However, BSP seems to lack any clear approach towards the organisation of this documentation and towards techniques which can be used to produce it.

There is no separately defined BSP project management method at this point in time. The working procedures provide certain points of control, but the linking of these points into any project management method remains the responsibility of the study team leader.

The BSP study activities themselves are described and a sample study work plan, complete with relevant control points, is given.

No mention is made of any possible connections to any other documentation or project management methods excepting the reference to IBM DB/DC Data Dictionary.

.4. Observations

BSP seems to be a good, practical methodology, especially when combined with other suitable documentation and project control methods.

Perhaps the most useful facility that could be added to BSP would be a method for the control and management of the follow-on project activities. This would greatly aid BSP's aim of defining and implementing IRM functions which support the company's business processes.

54

References.

1. Business System Planning - "Information System Planning Guide", IBM Corporation, Technical Publications/Industry, New York, 1975.

2. Business System Planning - Second Edition, October 1978.

3. EDP-Analyzer - June 1979, Vol 17, no. 6.

4. Meredith, F. - Business System Planning in SEAS 1978, Session Report.

5. Sebus, G.M.W. - "Business Systems Planning" Informatie, Vol 23, no. 3, Amsterdam, March 1981.

6. Business System Planning - Third Edition, July 1981.

3.2. SADT (Structured Analysis and Design Technique).

.1. Outline of the methodology.

.1.1. Philosophy.

SADT is a methodology with the aim to assist in the production of a correct requirements specification and, consequently, a good systems design.
The SADT philosophy is based on common sense and the design experience that its authors gathered from some twenty years of experience in setting up manufacturing operations. Nowadays, there is a considerable amount of SADT experience in the computing industry.
An essential element in SADT is that before a problem can be solved, it must be properly defined. The problem is defined in a model using a notation consisting of boxes and arrows. This model acts as an easy-to-read blueprint which enables all people concerned in the design process to participate in the process of constructing the requirements definitions.
The modelling principles are based on the idea that systems can be defined by relating things (data) and happenings (activities) and that this is similar, for example, to natural languages which relate nouns and verbs to form useful expressions.

Because of the fact that the solution to a problem which is incorrectly (or partial incorrectly) formulated is not benificial to an organisation, the philosophy of the methodology emphasises this requirements definition. After the requirements are defined, a framework is created for the systems architecture design phase followed by the programming, testing and implementation phases.

Requirements definition consists of the following aspects:

a. Context analysis

What does the environment of the problem look like and what are the relations between problem and environment.

b. <u>Functional specifications</u>

What functions have to be implemented and what
are the boundary conditions to take into account
in the design phase.

c. <u>Design constraints</u>

What are the constraints on how the required
system is to be built and implemented.

In addition to providing a clear definition of
the problem, the systems requirements definition
aims at the construction of a framework which
will facilitate successful, independent execution
of the following phase of systems design. The
difficulty here is to judge the level of detail
necessary. It must be sufficient to ensure that
the specification of the following phase is
unambiguous and yet brief enough to provide a
clear, concise overview.

Each of the aspects mentioned above can be
analysed from three different viewpoints e.g.
   -technical, the system architecture
   -operational, or how does the system fit into
    its environment. This includes such things as
    constraints on response times and elapsed
    times as well as considerations of organisa-
    tional impact
   -economic, or cost/benefit analysis.

The aspects and viewpoints can be put together,
as in fig. 3.2.1.

Viewpoints \ Aspects	Technical assessment	Operational assessment	Economic assessment
Context analysis	Current operations	Problem statement	Sensitivity factors
Functional specification	Proposed functions	Performance parameters	Expected impacts
Design constraints	Resource spec's	Usage conditions	Expected costs

<u>Figure 3.2.1</u> : Relating aspects of requirements
                definitions to viewpoints.

Defining the requirements is done by people and in order to make this process succesfull, all participants have a thorough knowledge of the subject, the documentation system, the participants roles and the way in which the analysis is performed.

A methodology, which assists in defining requirements should:

- give a good understanding of the real-world "system"
- have a good easy-to-read documentation system
- have a process for problem analysis with well defined roles for the participants and effective procedures for communication
- show how the process is to be managed technically in order to ensure that the specifications are stated clearly and the design (i.e. the solution) is moved to the next phase.

SADT describes these four points as follows.

a. <u>System</u>

A system can be defined as consisting of things which generate activities related to other things; each such activity is called a happening.

In order to maintain a proper distinction of the technical (computer view) and material (user view) aspects during the stage of defining the requirements, the concept of functional requirements is introduced. Functional requirements comprise the list of all happenings and related things which form the system.
System architecture comprises technical matters such as hardware configuration, record lay-outs, file descriptions, terminal networks, job runs, etc.

Setting the requirements definitions means establishing the functional architecture, explaining why this architecture was chosen and formulating the boundary conditions in which the system is to be designed.
The requirements definitions are established by means of the top-down approach.

b. Documenting

As medium of communication for all participants, a form of documentation is required that can be easily read and understood.
The documentation produced must be capable of providing a complete overview of the whole system, showing all relevant relationships, as well as giving a good insight into system requirements at a detailed level.
Based on the documentation all participants must be able to do desk-checking in order to ensure that any omissions are revealed as soon as possible.

The final form of the requirements definition should be considered as a contract between users and the software development staff.

c. The analysis process

The analysis for the requirements definition is carried out by a team that consists of people with very different back-grounds.
Team members are customers, users, management, designers, information analysists.
This team generates ideas, alternatives and requirements and the results will be different models from different viewpoints.

SADT does not demand a complete corporate information plan as a starting point. Its methods can be fitted into the context in which the problem is to be solved.

d. Managing the process

During the process of analysis one has to take care that the subject does not fall into pieces which are no longer related to each other, and that every step follows logically from the preceding step. To achieve this, the following questions have to be asked at each checkpoint: what are we doing, why do we do that and how will we continue from here. Adequate technical management makes sure that these questions are asked at the right times.

Another task of the project manager is to ensure
that the problem is not described in too much
detail at too early a stage. If this happens that
overall picture can become blurred by confusing
details.

Good systems development requires walk-throughs,
reviews and configurations management.
An essential concept in SADT-project management
is that only written agreements and comments will
be taken into account.

.1.2. <u>The working procedure</u>

The working procedure and documentation method
(see .1.3.) can hardly be separated within SADT:
the creation of the documentation is naturally
imbedded in the analysis process.

For the working procedure and the documentation a
special language is constructed called Structured
Analysis (SA).

The problem is represented by the SA-language in
several models. A model describes a subject from
one viewpoint with one purpose.
A viewpoint is an aspect of the subject that is
valuable as starting point for performing an
analysis (for instance the viewpoint of management, or of a specific user) and the purpose is
given by the audience for whom we make the
analysis and with whom we want to discuss the
result.

Since every subject has more than one aspect and
also more than one audience, a number of SA-
models will result. These models may be
overlapping or may be contradictory at certain
points, but since they have been derived from the
same basic set of facts, they can subsequently be
linked together.
The working procedure may be summarised as follows: when agreement is reached on the initial
subject, a top-down approach is used to break
this subject down into a maximum of six sub-
subjects. Then each subject itself will be decomposed into parts and so on (see figure 3.2.2).

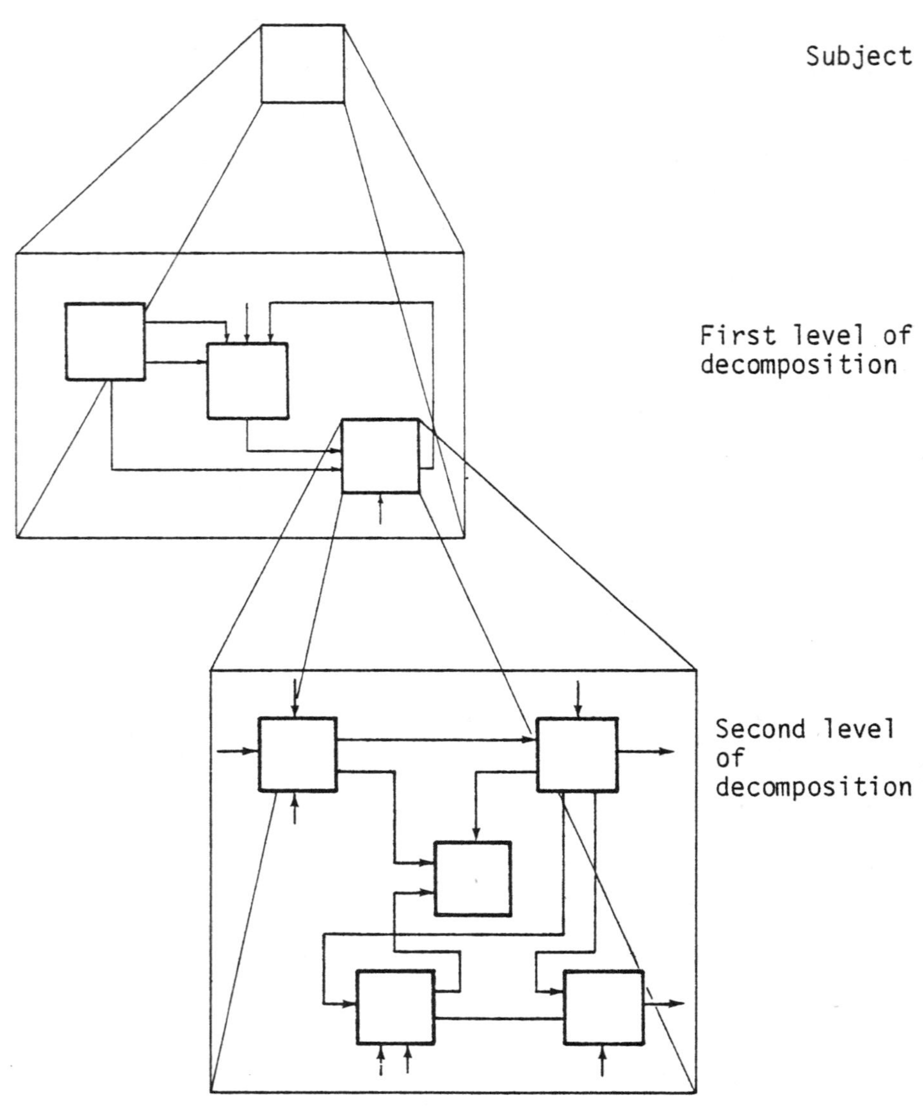

Figure 3.2.2. Structured decomposition.

This process of decomposition results in a number
of diagrams. The structured collation of diagrams
is called the SA-model.
Each decomposition results in a maximum of six
parts; the number six is derived from experience.

The process of decomposition goes on until a
complete insight into the problem to be analysed
is gained. As stated before in .1.1, the
detailing should not go any deeper then strictly
necessary for the stage of the study.

The top-down approach will not, formally, be
followed by a bottom-up return.

In the SA-language every problem can be analysed
in two ways: one that emphasises on the
happenings and one that emphasises the things in
a system. In order to be able to check the
completeness of the analysis, it is recommended
to perform both the activity (happenings) and
data (things) analysis.

The SA-language has 40 features. Each feature
consists of the following aspects: purpose (for
example: relating), concept (from/to), mechanism
(arrow) and notation (label).
Some features and concepts are listed in the
table of figure 3.2.3.

SADT distinguishes the steps: systems requirements, design, building (programming and testing) and implementation.

Before using SADT, the methodology has to be introduced into the organisation. There are no standard techniques for introduction, so each company must determine its own techniques. The best way to become acquainted with the practical aspects of SADT is to gain the necessary know-ledge and experience by using it in a project environment. The theoretical techniques can be learnt in a short space of time. However the training is simple and does not make the user aware of all potential practical problems.
Before a project is started, all proposed proce-dures and appointments have to be integrated with the documentation method in order to decide what documentation is to be produced at which stage of the analysis process.

Purpose	Concept		Mechanism	Notation	
Bound context	Inside/outside		SA-box	Name	
Relate/ connect	From/to		SA-arrow	Label	
Name	Activity data		SA-names	Activity data	
	Happenings	Things		Verb	Noun
Label	Things	Happenings	SA-labels	Noun	Verb
Show dominance	Control	Input	Constraint		
Show relevance	I.C.O.	I.C.O.	All interfaces		

Figure 3.2.3 Some features of the SA-language

.1.3. <u>Documentation method</u>

The documentation method is an essential part of the SA-language and therefore of the SADT-methodology.
Graphically, one starts with a diagram that represents the subject to be analysed. Then the diagram is broken down into another diagram that consists of boxes and arrows which connect the boxes. Subsequently each of the boxes can be decomposed into boxes in a next diagram and so on.

The boxes may represent activities (happenings) or data (things). When they represent activities the horizontal arrows indicate the interfaces between the boxes and of special importance are the inputs (the arrows at the left side) needed for the activity, and the outputs (the arrows at the right side) produced by the activity. The top vertical arrows represent the external factors that control the activity of the box, and the mechanism arrows at the bottom show the support.
When the boxes represent data, the horizontal arrows show the transactions (activities) that have transformed, or will transform the data, the top vertical arrows indicate the constraints on the use or creation of the data, and the bottom arrow shows the storage medium.

The labelling of the diagrams, boxes and the changes caused by the arrows, have to be stated in clear, simple words.
Above these, if necessary, a brief explanation can be added, though this explanation may not replace the function of the diagram.

Figure 3.2.4 gives an example of a box and arrow representation. An example, in which the SA-language describes itself, can be found in reference 2.

The total set of diagrams serves to set out both the complete systems requirements and the systems design in a global and in a detailed way.
The SADT methodology does not say how the diagrams are to be numbered, who should read which diagram or when a diagram is officially accepted. These matters should, however, be agreed upon before the project is started.

.1.4. Project management method

For the participants in the process of defining the requirements and setting up the design, the following roles have to be fulfilled:

Authors

Staff who study the requirements specifications and constraints, who will analyse the functions and draw up the SADT-diagrams.

Commentors

These people review the work of the authors, and give written comments on their work. These comments also apply to the models and may include a number of alternatives. Commentors often perform the role of authors in other parts of the project.

Readers

Personnel who study the SADT-diagrams. Their comments are usually restricted to verifying the completeness and accuracy of the work done.

Experts

Persons, who are contacted by authors and who give expert advice about requirements and constraints.

Technical committee

A group consisting of senior technical staff who review the decomposition at each level and either resolve technical issues or give advice about them to the project management.

Project librarian

This person is responsible for the central SADT-files containing all documents. He makes copies, distributes them to readers, keeps records, etc.

Project manager

He is responsible for the technical conduct of the systems analysis and design.

Chief analyst

A participant on a temporary basis who assists in implementing the SADT-methodology.

Instructor

A person who trains the other participants of the project.

The exact contents of the task of each staff member, as well as the project organisation, depend on the company organisation and on the subject, and have to be established at the beginning of the project.

As mentioned before, at various points in time, reviews and walk-throughs will take place.

.2. <u>Evaluation matrix SADT</u>

		philosophy	working procedure	documentation method			project-management method
				tech	org	cont	
Company analysis/ synthesis	1.1						
	1.2						
	1.3						
project-selection							
Logical design	3.1	▨	▨	▨		▨	
	3.2	▨	▨	▨		▨	
Logical → technical	4.1	▨	▨	▨		▨	
	4.2	▨	▨	▨		▨	
Technical design	5.1						
	5.2						
Physical design	6.1						
	6.2						
	6.3						
	6.4						
implementation							
exploitation							

.3.   <u>Applicability of the methodology</u>

.3.1.   <u>Description of the matrix coverage</u>

The methodology is suitable for the analysis of happenings and of things and, for reasons of completeness, it is advisable to carry out the decompositions both for the activities and the data.

The methodology is specially designed for the phases of company analysis, synthesis and logical design and may well also be helpful in the transformation to the technical design.

It is doubtful whether the methodology is very suitable for the analysis of the organisational aspects of the company information model.

The methodology does not give criteria on methods for project selection, though some models may be constructed from the viewpoints of project selection in the preceding phase.

Since SADT is not focussed on the technical aspects, i.e. system architecture, the methodology will only assist partially in the technical design phase.

From this technical design phase onwards, other methodologies are probably to be preferred, although SADT should not be completely excluded.

.3.2. <u>Thoroughness of the methodology</u>

The methodology aims at, and provides the tools to achieve, a clear definition of the subject problem. This definition acts as a starting point for fruitful, independent development in the next project phase.
The documentation methods provide for the specification of a clear overview as well as all relevant details. The methodology allows the subject to be analysed from all relevant "viewpoints" and for all relevant "purposes". It recommends that both processes of data and activity analysis be carried out.

From the viewpoint of avoiding ambiguity and mis-interpretation the uniform method of documentation is a great advantage.

.3.3. Row transition

As said in .3.1., when used during the phase of company analysis, the SADT-analysis carried out from the relevant viewpoints could serve as input for the project selection phase.

The analysis of the logical design phase should be carried out as natural continuation of the analysis during the first phase.
The result of the logical design can easily be used for the transformation phase.

.3.4. Column coordination

The aspects of philosophy, working procedure and documentation method are well integrated. SADT, however, does not offer a clear project management method. It rather creates an environment which induces a certain way of structured thinking. This certainly aids in the implementation of an optimal approach to project development.
If it is to be successfully applied, SADT also requires that documentation procedures are enforced, review points are systematically planned and all decisions are written down.

3.2.4. Observations

In using a methodology within an organisation, one can recognise the following problems:

- the necessary changes of mentality for the analyst (the emphasis lies on what is done rather than how it is done) are not easily realised

- a considerable effort is required for education and training

- users must also be educated and trained

- there are no practical, uniform guidelines

concerning levels of detail i.e. how far activities and data should be decomposed

- the preparation period takes time and makes
  management impatient ("when do they really
  start?").

Specific SADT problems are:

- the availability of the knowledge of the SADT-
  methodology originates from two kinds of
  sources: articles and lectures (on which this
  article is based) and patented courses (given
  by Softech)

- sometimes it is difficult to add sufficient
  nuances in the arrows

- the drawing technique requires a lot of time

- the written communication procedures cost a
  lot of time and diminish flexible communication

- keeping the documentation up-to-date requires
  a lot of time from a lot of highly trained
  people.

SADT can be connected to the PSL/PSA-system.
PSL/PSA then serves as a data dictionary for
SADT, and assists in assuring the consistency,
allocation and diagramming of the requirements.

In practice some 20 of the available 40 SADT-
features are used.

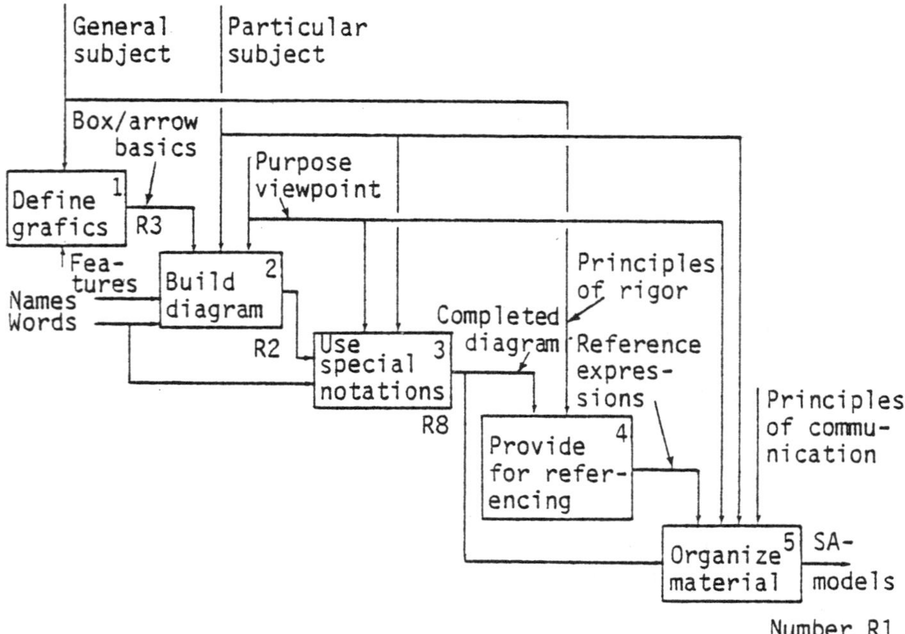

Figure 3.2.4.: Example of box and arrow presentation
(first level of the description of the
SA-laguage).

References

1. Douglas T. Ross, Kenneth E. Schoman Jr. — Structured Analysis for Requirements Definitions, IEEE Transactions on Software Engineering, Vol. SE-3 , no. 1, January 1977

2. Douglas T. Ross — Structured Analysis (SA): A Language for communicating ideas, IEEE Transactions on Software Engineering, Vol. SE-3. no. 1, January 1977.

3. — The Analysis of User Needs, EDP Analyzer, Vol. 17, no. 1, January 1979

4. P. Bernus — Computer Aids to the Design of Integrated Manufacturing Systems, Computers in Industry 1, July 1979.

5. Ralph I. Rudkin Kenneth D. Shere — Structured Decomposition Diagram, A new technique for system analysis. Datamation, October 1979.

6. L.A. Maarssen and C.L. McGowan — Ontwikkelingsmethoden 12. Structured Analysis and Design Technique (SADT), Informatie 7 & 8, juli/augustus 1981.

3.3 ISAC

.1. Outline of the methodology

Although ISAC is a self-contained methodology, it is perhaps especially important because various ISAC ideas have been borrowed by methodologies. For example, MOS and SASO use many ISAC-type concepts and diagrams, and a strong relationship exists between ISAC and the Jackson Structured Programming methodology. Although we have described ISAC in our own terminology, we have taken some of the diagrams and definitions directly from the ISAC methodology description itself.

.1.1. Philosophy

The ISAC method (Information Systems work and Analysis of Changes) has been developed by a research group at the department of Administrative Information Processing of the Royal Institute of Technology, and the University of Stockholm, Sweden.

The method aims at a new approach to the development of informations systems. In this approach the analysis and design phases are emphasized.
The group has been working since 1971 and consists amongst others of M. Lundeberg, G. Goldkuhl and A. Nillson (1).

The "analysis and design" of information systems is divided in four areas:

activity analysis

> problem oriented work

information analysis

equipment adaptation

> data oriented work

data system design

As a definition of the term information system is
given:
- "a system that has been developed to create,
choose, collect, store, process, distribute and
interpret information".
Information is characterized as knowledge or
addition to knowledge, represented by data.

"An information system can thus also be seen as
an organised co-operation between people in order
to process and convey information to each other".
In the "analysis and design", therefor all participants should be involved.

The ISAC method (1) consists of a working procedure that starts from the needs, problems and
ideas as experienced by users, and that ends with
final specifications for manual routines and computer programs. The method consists of the execution of a number of controllable and coherent
steps. Rules are given to explain which ISAC modules are applicable and what documentation should
be produced during those steps. The development
of information systems is thus placed in a broader context:

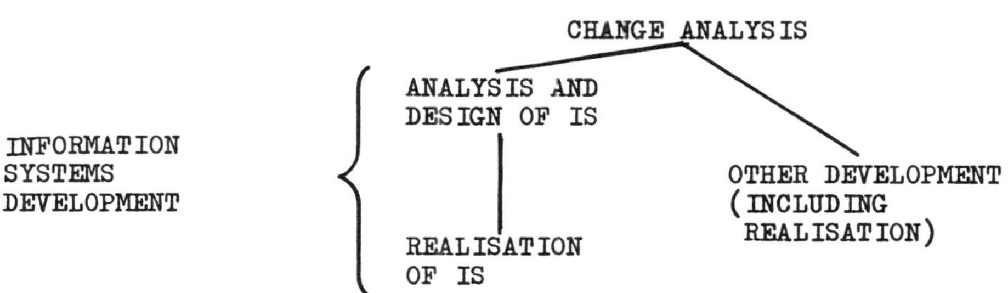

Figure 3.3.1 Development of information systems.

The method advocates the use of a cooperative
structure in which users, problem oriented system
analysts and data oriented system designers

participate in the development process. ISAC also pays attention to the following human aspects:
- the communication process
- the learning process
- change strategies
- project administration approaches.

The methodology is based on a top down philosophy which starts with a "change analysis". In this first phase, current activities (or processes) and desired changes are described. The total information system is then partitioned into information subsystems each of which can be evaluated from the point of view of development feasibility and the anticipated cost/benefit results. This partitioning is accompanied by a definition of the sets of input and output messages which relate all subsystems.

The idea is to match each user work situation with the information system (or subsystem) needed to produce the relevant information.
ISAC identifies three different change analysis strategies, namely:
- process strategy, based upon the idea that users themselves formulate and solve their problems in a change strategy whereby specialists (acting as catalysts) can help.
- expert strategy, based upon the solution of problems by external experts.
  This solution is "sold" to users afterwards.
- anchoring strategy, which falls in between the former two. This means that multi disciplined working groups are formed to provide solutions and to implement them.
The last strategy is advocated by ISAC.

The following ISAC statements are worth mentioning:
  1. the users can control the development of in-formation systems themselves.
  2. information systems development can be per-formed in a number of small, manageable and interrelated steps.
  3. in the development process, it is possible to achieve good cooperation between different professional disciplines.
  4. maintenance and modification of an information system can be done in an effective and secure way.

5. development of information systems can become a natural part of the normal activities of the users.
6. the problem oriented systems analyst can function as a catalyst.
7. the data oriented systems designer can concentrate on developing the technical data design.
8. the information system can be evaluated extensively in advance, and thus become well anchored in the organisation.
9. during the development process, equal emphasis can, and should, be placed on the different analysis and design areas.
10. a crude measure of the successfullness of an information system development project might be formulated as follows: "degree of success = f (quality * acceptance)"

.1.2. Working procedure

The ISAC working procedure consists of two main sets of actions to be performed (two-stage rocket), namely the problem oriented and the data oriented sets of actions.
This procedure can be roughly drawn as follows:

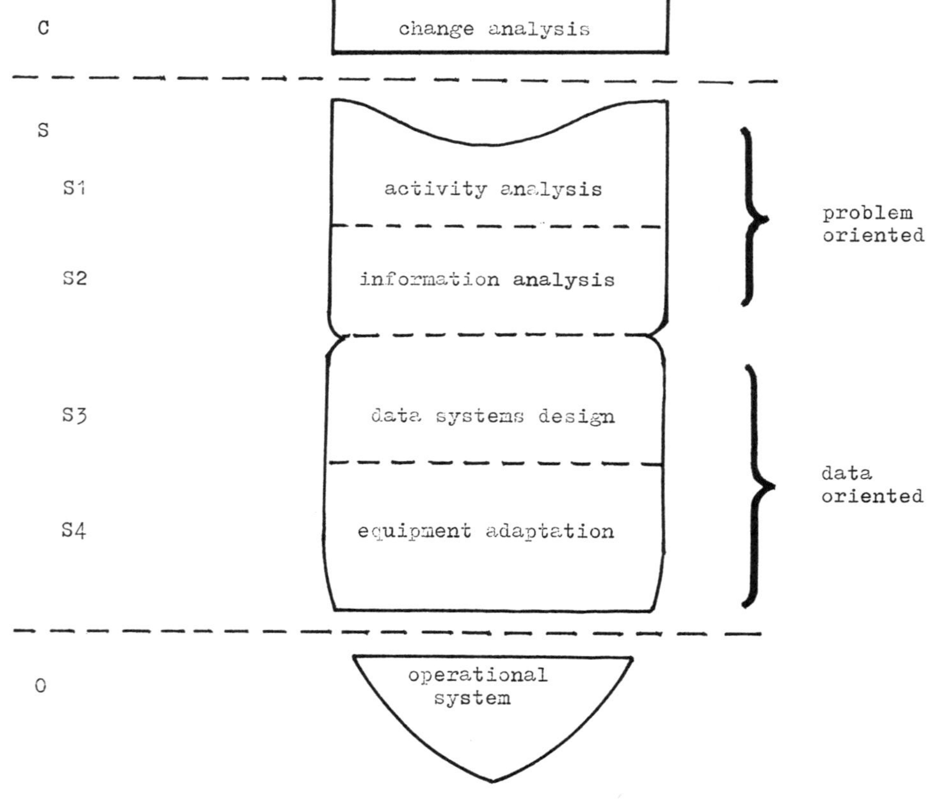

Figure 3.3.2. "Two stage rocket".

.1.2.1. Change Analysis

This is the first phase of the ISAC methodology. It aims to investigate the changes and improvements which have to be made in order to ensure the efficient operation of the companies business activities. This means that all relevant problems and needs must be identified and investigated. It is seen as important to diagnose the reasons behind the problems, and not simply to treat the more obvious symptoms. This demands a combination of development tools which can support the evaluation of social, human and economic factors.

Systems development is only considered when change analysis shows that certain problems and needs are related to information handling. Examples of possible solutions other than systems development are:
- product development
- improvements to the physical production or distribution systems
- organisational changes
- improvements in the areas of personnel relations e.g. communications training.

In the following text, the change analysis steps are described in chronological sequence. In practice, a number of iterations become necessary because later steps can give rise to new knowledge or perspectives which impact work done in the earlier steps (see the ISAC scheme of figure 3.3.4).
Change analysis can be divided into:
c1 analysis of problems and needs
c2 study of change alternatives
c3 choice of change approach
This also requires a study of the relationships that exist between these activities, the people involved and their problems or desires for change.

c1.1 Problem listing
Current and anticipated problems are documented in a problem table.

c1.2 Analysis of interest groups
Interpretation of the problem table leads to the identification of the interest groups (personnel categories) that are affected by the problems

listed. Some examples are given in the ISAC documentation.
These groups are listed in an <u>interest group table</u>. The combination of the problem table and the interest group table may indicate how a suitable change strategy could be formulated, or how an existing change strategy could be modified.

c1.3 Problem grouping
Problems are arranged in a number of groups and documented in a <u>problem groups table</u>. These groups may form the basis for (sub) projects to be specified later on.

c1.4 Description of current activities.
The relevant activities are now described in relation with the problems and the interest groups. To do this, an activity model is produced using the SDA technique (Systematic Description of Activities, Nissen-Andersen, 1978). Such an activity model consists of <u>A-graphs, text pages</u> and <u>property tables</u>.

The extent of this description is relative to the level of detail of the analysis and evaluation in step c1.6. An example of an A-graph is given in figure 3.3.3. (ISAC Change Analysis in an A-graph).
The A-graphs (activity schema) have a hierarchical structure in order to provide a better overview of the complex activities.
This structure also serves to give a better insight into the details of the activities. Quantitative and qualitative properties of the activities have to be described. These are documented in <u>property tables</u>.

c1.5 Description and analysis of objectives
In this step, the needs are 'translated' into a number of realistic objectives. The aim of further development work is to realise these objectives. They are documented in a <u>table of objectives</u>. This translation is regarded as a difficult but important step by ISAC.

c1.6 Analysis and evaluation of current situation
The needs, desires (as in the table of objectives) and the current situation ("IST" and "SOLL" situation) are now compared.

This analysis is followed by an evaluation. The problems to be solved are prioritized according to the values assigned by the different interest groups. The problems can then be transformed into needs for change.

c2. Study of change alternatives
Different change aternatives are now generated and described. These alternatives are evaluated from human, social and economic viewpoints. In general, this generation and evaluation is performed for each of the problem groups.

c2.1 Generation, creation of alternatives
This is considered the creative part by ISAC and therefor no 'exact' guidelines are given. A systematic investigation of flows and activities which may be subject to changes may be of help. The results are described in a table of change alternatives.

c2.2. Description of change alternatives
In order to analyse and evaluate the consequences of changes, each change alternative is described by means of a new activity model. This model consists of an A-graph accompanied by a textual description and a property table.

c2.3 Analysis and evaluation of the change alternatives
Analysis and evaluation of the change alternatives is performed with regard to human, social and economic factors. This provides the basic information for making an appropriate choice between the change alternatives.

c3. Choice of change approach
The third and last step of the change analysis consists of the choice of the proper change alternative and the determination of development measures suitable for each problem group. The relationships between changes which may be performed in parallel are also considered.

c3.1 Choice of change alternative
The reasons behind this choice are documented.

c3.2 Choice of development measures
One change alternative leads to a combination of

measures to be taken such as development of company activitities, of information systems, of the organisation and education of personnel. The choices and the reasons for it are documented.

<u>c3.3 Analysis of parallel development measures</u>
Finally the parallel measures and their mutual influences are investigated on three levels:
- .different measures within the same problem group
- .relationships between problem groups within one area of activities
- .circumstances that affect other areas of activities.

The final result of the change analysis consists of models of the current and the possible future situations. The models are analysed with respect to human, social and economic factors.
Additionally, a plan for further development of the organisation etc. results.
An example in the ISAC-documentation (1) illustrates the change analysis.

N.B.	Figure 3.3.3 is an activity graph which attempts to describe change analysis using the ISAC-methodology itself. It proves that the change analysis activities are not described to such extent that a fully consistent schema can be derived.

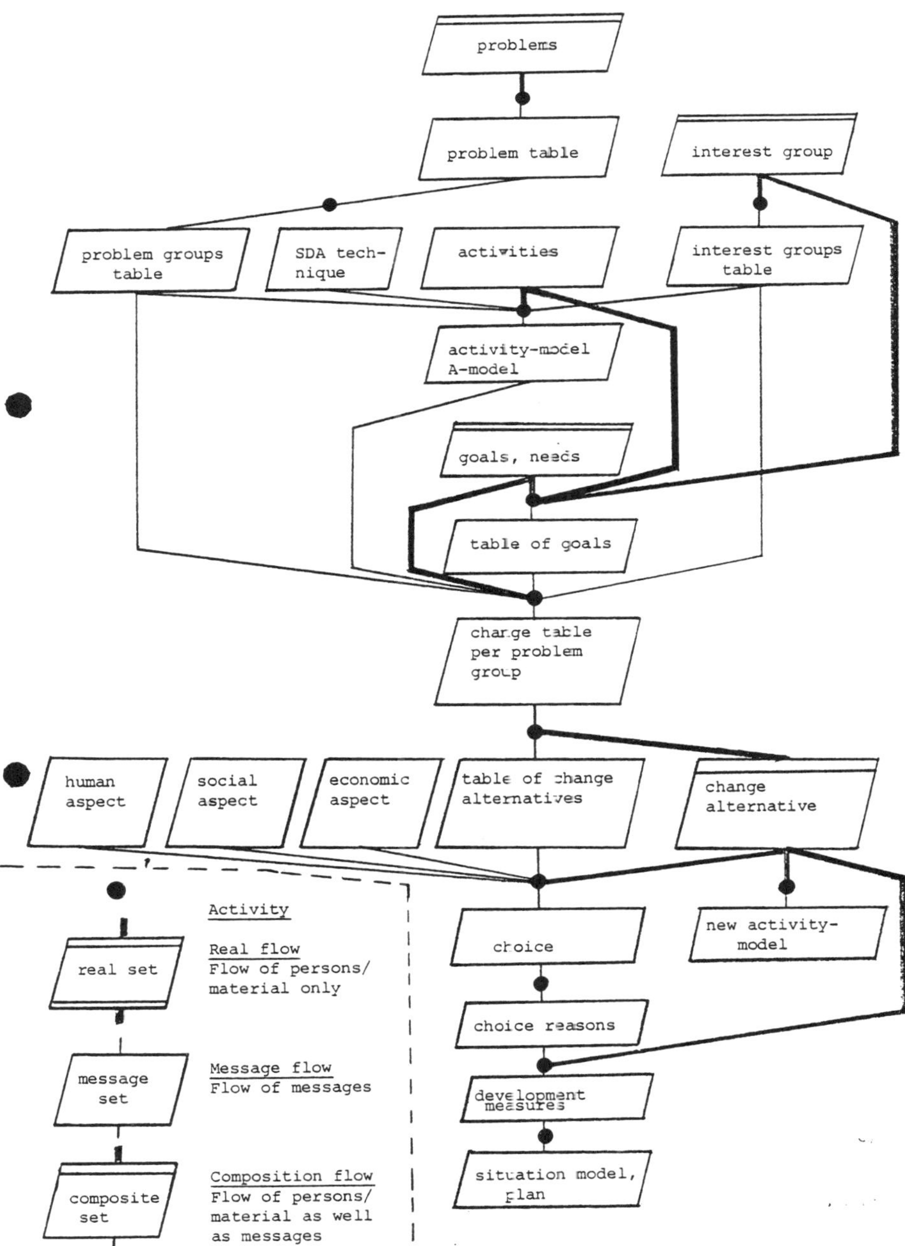

Figure 3.3.3 ISAC-change analysis in an activity -graph (red.)

1.2.2 Problem oriented work

The next step in the analysis phase is problem oriented. This involves the activity analysis (A-actions) and the information analysis (I-actions) studies:

S.1.   Activity analysis
S.2.   Information analysis.

S.1. Activity studies

The analysis of activities is subdivided into:
- partitioning of information subsystems
                                        , S.1.1.
- study of information subsystem
                                        , S.1.2.
- coordination between information subsystems
                                        , S.1.3.

S.1.1. Partitioning into information subsystems

Only when information system needs are identified by change analysis an activity study is performed. This study starts with the description of the information processing which takes place in the previously identified activities (processes, red.).

S.1.1.1. Detailed description of activities

The activity models described during the change analysis represent a rough picture of the activities within the selected change alternative. It is supposed that part of the chosen change alternative is the recommendation to develop new information systems, or to modify existing information systems. These systems have to be described as parts of the (company-) activities using A-graphs, textual descriptions, and property tables.

S.1.1.2. Identification of information subsystems

In this step all A-graphs are analyzed to detect potential information subsystems. The candidate subsystems are documented in a preliminary-list of information systems. The approach is based on defining several information subsystems, as opposed to one total system. Specific information systems that provide relevant information for the users in their worksituation are identified.

S.1.1.3. Classification of information systems

The identified subsystems are grouped with regard to their "formalizability, automatability and type of processing". Four different types of information processing activities are outlined:

- IS1, non-formalizable (e.g. informal contacts and knowledge): these systems are necessarily "manual",
- IS2, formalizable but non-automatable (e.g. standardised telephone calls, mail procedures),
- IS3, automatable with calculations that can be performed according to fixed rules. During data systems design it is decided whether tasks are to be executed manually or with the aid of computers or other technical tools.
- IS4, automatable with only message transport in time (storage) or space (switching). This form of message transport is easy to formalise. The way in which this will be performed is decided upon in the data system design.

S.1.1.4. Delimitation of information subsystems

The description of the activities (A-graphs etc.) is now transformed in such a way that information subsystems occur as delimited activities within the A-graphs. This delimitation per subsystem is achieved by defining "sets of input and output messages".

The description of the activities is carried out to a level where the sets of output messages of a subsystem:

- are similar in nature (comparable) to the user e.g. concern similar objects and events in the activities of the organisation.
- have comparable time requirement (response time, frequency, etc.). A practical distinction is made between manual and automatable systems. The automatable systems will result in separate subsystems.

S.1.2. Study of information subsystems

Each information subsystem is considered with regard to costs and benefits. Alternative "ambition levels" are generated and tested. Finally a suitable level is chosen.

S.1.2.1. Analysis of contributions

In this step some of the procedures outlined in change analysis are repeated. The purpose is to determine the interaction between the proposed subsystem and the relevant activities. This may necessitate further detailed elaboration of these activities in order to see how the information generated by the subsystem under consideration is used by these activities. In this way it should be possible to determine the contribution which the proposed information system can make towards the fulfillment of the goals of the people involved in the various activities. The contributions (benefits) are documented in a <u>property table</u>.

S.1.2.2. Generation of alternative levels of ambition

The choice of levels of ambition is influenced by two factors:
- the quality of the information to be delivered, the possibility to specify calculation rules, the average and maximum workload.
- requirements for response time, timeliness, frequency, volume and confidentiality.

The choices are also documented in <u>property - tables</u>. Alternative levels of ambition are generated and documented in a <u>table of ambition-levels</u>.

S.1.2.3. Test of ambition levels

In this step the choices are checked to see if they are realisable e.g. by studying similar information systems which are operational elsewhere, or by a 'desk test' using the models, or by a 'field test' constructing a simplified prototype.

S.1.2.4 Cost/benefit analysis

A calculation of the benefits is a refinement of the contributions mentioned in S.1.2.1. Benefits are considered only during the activity study (S) while the costs are calculated in more detail in each successive development step. Here the costs are estimated roughly.

S.1.2.5. Choice of ambition level

By consideration of the human and social aspects of the change analysis and the cost/benefit

analysis results, a suitable ambition level is chosen.
N.B. The result at this stage may well be that the proposed information systems development is discontinued.

S.1.3. Coordination of information subsystems

This third step concludes the activity study. It deals with the analysis of the relations between the different informaton subsystems and the allocation of development priorities.

S.1.3.1. Analysis of relations between different information subsystems

Those systems to be considered for further development are listed. The relationships between these subsystems are described, analysed and documented.

S.1.3.2. Priority rating between different subsystems

Development resources are limited and therefor priorities have to be set for the order of systems development.
N.B. In the ISAC-documentation an example is inserted to illustrate the preceding development steps and to show how these steps may be performed.

S.2. Information analysis

Now the second phase of the problem oriented work is described. In this phase, the information analysis, the following steps have to be executed:

- precedence and component analysis; S.2.1.
- process analysis   ; S.2.2.
- property analysis   ; S.2.3.

The first two have to be executed in sequential order. The third one may be executed in parallel to the first two steps.

86

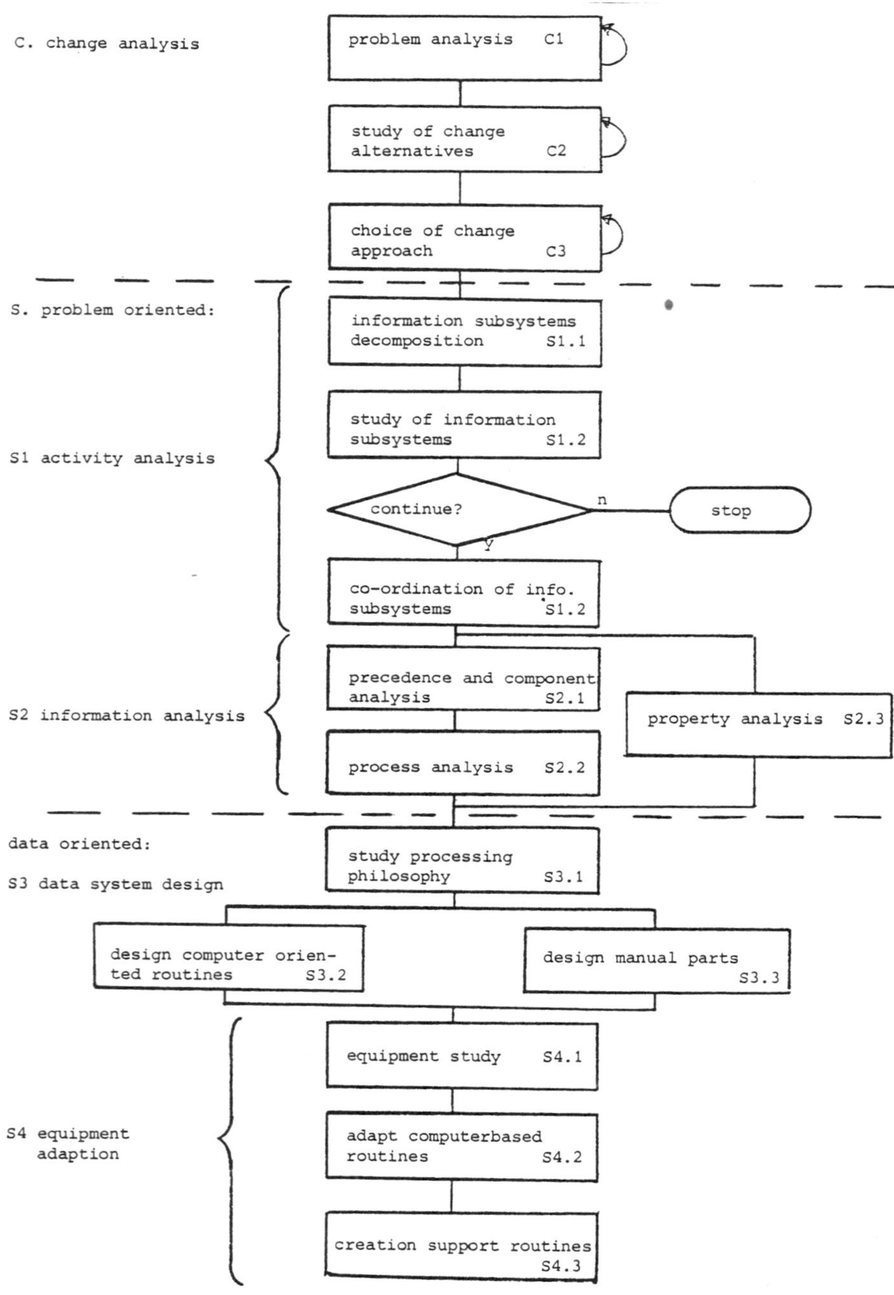

Figure 3.3.4. ISAC-working procedure in a graph

S.2.1. Precedence and component analysis

Precedence analysis deals with the analysis of the "information precedence relations" in an information system: the information sets necessary to derive a particular information set are analysed.
Component analysis consists of the analysis of the structure of these information sets: the message types (identification and properties) that 'describe' an information set are analysed.

S.2.1.1. Transition from activity studies

During the activity studies a number of subsystems are delineated by a rough description of input and output information sets. These subsystems are also classified in a list of information systems giving their formalisability, automatability and type of processing, together with the priorities allocated.

The goal and the extent of the information analysis now depends on the classification of the sybsystems.

When a subsystem is regarded as automatable, information analysis has to be performed. If the information subsystem is nonautomatable, the extent of information analysis appropriately varies from case to case. This first step is meant to decide on the extent of the information analysis. This is documented in an information analysis planning table.
For each subsystem the following transition steps are executed:

T1: extract from an A-graph of a subsystem the input and output information sets and put these in a I-schema (for the I-graph symbols see fig. 5).
T2: study the next pages of the A-graphs in order to achieve a more precise description of those sets.
T3: Refine the I-graph by means of precedence analysis.

For each subsystem an overall I-graph is set up. These graphs are identified by one or two prefix letters followed by a code.

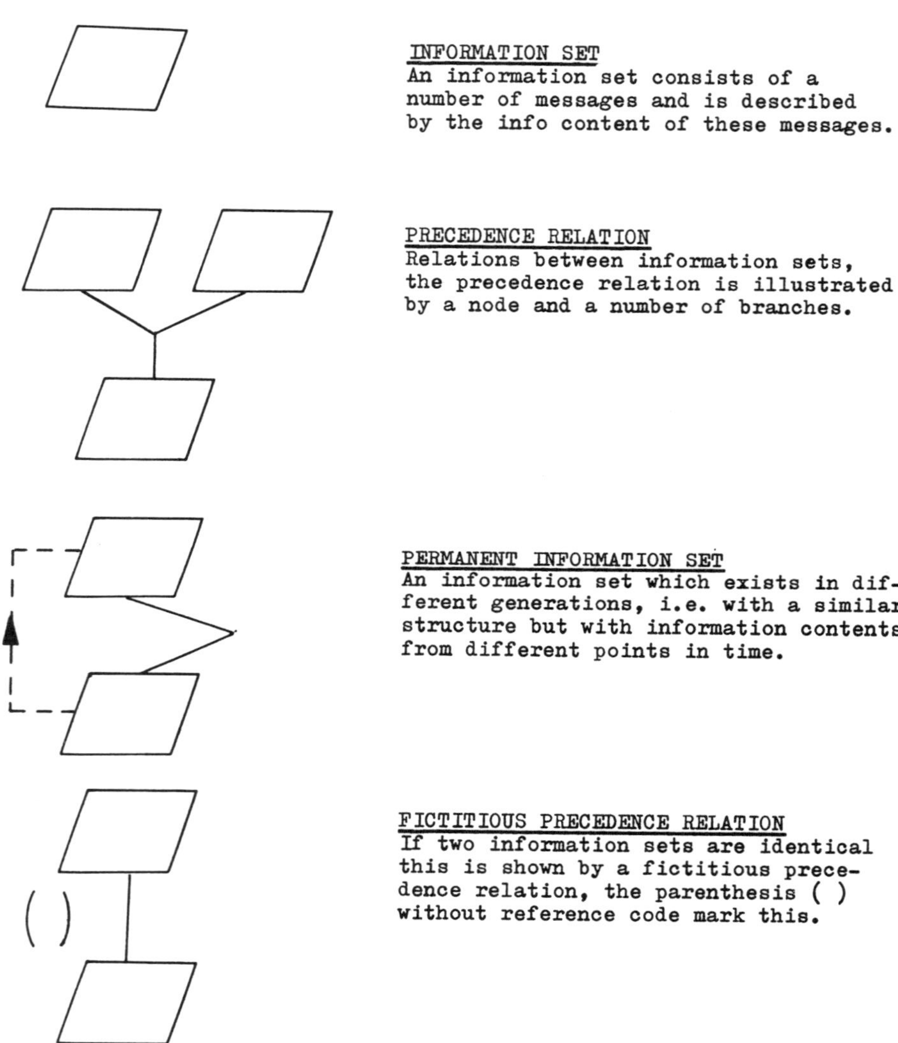

Figure 3.3.5. Symbols in I-graphs

ISAC recommends that the following precedence and component analyses be executed interactivily but that it is best to start with component analysis of the output information sets, in order to obtain a better basis for the precedence analysis.

S.1.2.1. Continued precedence analysis
Precedence analysis is the analysis of information precedence relations. These relations are documented using I-graphs and textual descriptions. This documentation is hierarchical.

The precedence analysis steps for one level (I-graph) are:

P1: identify the output information sets, as given in the above.
P2: divide these if necessary into information subsets (this should correspond to the first step of the component analysis).
P3: analyse the precedences for each information set.
P4: repeat P3 until the input set is reached.

The 'information processes' are disregarded during the precedence analysis to simplify the analysis work.

S.2.1.3. Continued component analysis
The structures of the information sets are analysed in this step. These are documented in C-graphs.

The steps in the component analysis are:

C1: identify suitable subsets of the information sets
C2: list all terms occurring in a message of the information set.
C3: analyse the property terms and the identification terms to which they are related.
C4: document this in a C-graph.
C5: the different terms are documented in a term catalogue.

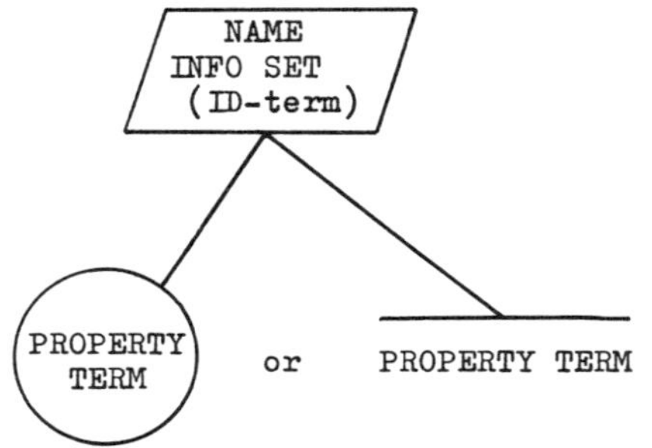

INFORMATION SET
Information set or subset. It is
given an information setname
followed by an identification term
in brackets. An ID-term is needed
for identification of relevant
material, events and people.

PROPERTY TERM
A property term means some form of
characterisation of material,
events or people.

Iteration (repetition)

Figure 3.3.6. Symbols in C-graphs

S.2.2. Process analysis

Process analysis is the detailed description of
the 'information processes' in the information
system. Processes are disregarded during
precedence analysis. Information precedence
relations form the nodes in the I-graphs.

S.2.2.1. Identification of information process

The processes are identified and listed in a
process list. Their 'reference codes' from the I-
graphs are used and they are given names.

S.2.2.2. Detailed description of information
processes

Each process is now described and the
descriptions are documented in process tables
(decision tables) that consist of
- prerequisites for the performance of a process
- calculations, conditions for alternative calculations and calculation rules.
In fact the descriptions say how the identifica-

tion and property terms of the output information sets are derived from corresponding terms of input information sets. The relations of a particular information process with other processes are not described. These are defined in C-graphs.

S.2.3. Property Analysis
Property analysis during information analysis is a continuation of the property descriptions formulated during the change analysis and the activity analysis.
The relevant property values are listed in property tables. ISAC distinguishes between a qualitative and a quantative property analysis.
N.B. An example in the ISAC-documentation attempts to illustrate the information analysis process.

.1.2.3. Data oriented work

This development work is divided into (see figure 3.3.2):
- data system design
- equipment adaptation.

S.3. Data system design

In this first phase of the data oriented work, ISAC distinguishes
- study of the processing philosophy   S.3.1
- design of computer-based routines   S.3.2
- design of manual parts   S.3.3

S.3.1. Study of the processing philosophy
This study consists of two methodology steps:
1. study of ways of processing
2. study of degree of centralization

S.3.1.1. Study of the ways of processing
In the activity studies, a distinction was made between manual and automatable parts of the information system. A final decision is now made as to which parts of the data system should be computer-based, automated in other ways (e.g. by use of microfiche) or manual. The data system may be partitioned into different ways of processing as follows:

1. The data system may be split into:
   - manual parts
   - manual parts with technical aids
   - automated parts
2. The automated parts may be:
   - computer-based parts
   - other automated parts
3. Finally, the computer-based parts may be subdivided into:
   - batch processing
   - direct, or real-time, processing.

In studying the ways of processing, the following three steps are used:

1. Combination of preliminary process collections. A preliminary process collection can correspond to:
   - an activity in a particular A-graph where only messages are processed.
   - an information process from the information analysis model
   - a natural group of information processes from the information analysis model.
2. Evaluation of the way of processing, whereby for each combination of preliminary process collections alternative ways of processing have to be described, analysed and evaluated.
3. Choice of the way of processing for each of the the parts of the data system. The result is documented in the <u>processing table</u>.

S.3.1.2. Study of degree of centralization

This study need only be done when several information systems are involved e.g. where multiple branches or departments are involved. The following steps are used:
1. Identification of philosophies of (de)centralization. An indication is given as to the necessity to perform each process collection centrally or locally. Since the number of potential combinations is large, it is often best to define a limited number of alternative philosophies which are sufficiently different from each other.

2. Supplementation with ways of transmission. For each alternative philosophy, data communication principles (or ways of

transmission) are specified e.g. using telex, mailing or telecommunications facilities. In complex cases, a technological outline of the communication facilities may be needed.

3. Evaluation of philosophies of (de)centralization. The alternative philosophies are evaluated against such factors as:
   - economic factors
   - service possibilities
   - reliability and availability
   - compatibility
   - backup possibilities
   - portability
   - flexibility
   - social effects
   - consequences for other data systems and their technical solutions.
   The results of the evaluation are documented in an <u>evaluation table.</u>

4. Choice of philosophy cf (de)centralization. The evaluation table results are used to make a choice of philosophy and this choice is documented in a processing table.

<u>S.3.2. Design of computer-based routines</u>
This design is done in two steps
- data structure design and program delimitation
- program design.

The first step is performed as follows:

1. Initial data system cocrdination.
   The structure of the data system and the relations between subsystems (in the form of datasets) are defined. The results are documented in <u>D-graphs</u> (data system design graphs). For symbols in D-graphs see ISAC (1) or (3).

2. Analysis of process collections.
   The combinations of preliminary process collections (S.3.1.) are now considered, and possibly subdivided, depending on frequencies and time requirements.

3. Analysis of permanent datasets.
   Because the datasets determine the structure

of the data system a thorough analysis of the different alternatives for permanent datasets is required. This analysis can be performed in two different ways: output analysis and input analysis.
The output analysis deals with the use of datasets to provide fast and secure accessibility. The input analysis deals with the updating of stored datasets:
addition, modification and deletion.
Factors to be considered here are:
consolidation, sort orders, access methods and search paths.
The result is the basis for the next step.

4. Generation of proposals for data structure design and program delimitation. This is another creative part of the design process. Alternative solutions for data structures and program boundaries have to be found. Within processing collections, data processes are grouped into programs. Data processing processes are defined e.g. sorting process, logging routines and security routines for system failures.
The alternatives are documented in <u>detailed D-graphs</u>, <u>in list of program/processes</u> and <u>in dataset tables</u>.

5. Evaluation and choice of proposed data structure design and program delimitation. After evaluation, a choice is made from the alternative solutions. This choice is documented.

The second step in the design of computer-based routines is program design (PD). It is performed on a machine independent level. Machine dependent properties of output and input data have to be bypassed here.
The program design approach of ISAC is based on the Jackson structured programming methodology. A reference is made to the research project MIDAS, a cooperation between the ISAC-group and SAAB-SCANIA, where Jackson's method was integrated with ISAC's information analysis (1976).

Data and programs are described similarly with the aid of three basic components: sequence, iteration, selection. Program design is performed in the following three steps:

1. Program-oriented data structure analysis.
   The input and output data for each program are described. This description forms the basis for the program control structure: the data description is thus program oriented. This program-oriented data structure and analysis is done as follows:
   PD1: For output and input data, list the following:
       -iterations (program independent). See C-graphs and property tables.
       -data technical existence selections (program independent). Such a selection is a special iteration with only zero or one element.
       -property selections based on the conditions described in the calculation parts of the information process descriptions.
       -possible sequences of data, derived from I-graphs and dataset descriptions.
   PD2: Group these structural elements in program oriented data structures. They are documented in D-structures using Jackson's notation.
   PD3: Analyse corespondence between the numbers and the order of the datasets. Supplement the D-structures with file selections. In this way all D-structures can be made to be consistent with each other.
       The result of this data structure analysis is documented in D-structures.

2. Design of control structure.
   This structure describes the control functions of each program. In the data structure analysis all control functions have been identified The "union" of the different D-structures forms the control structure of the program. This is documented in a P-structure (program structure).

3. Listing and allocation of operations.
   The control structure is only part of the complete program structure. Program operations must also be listed and allocated in the control structure.
   The result of the program design is a P-structure with allocated program operations.

S.3.3. Design of manual parts

In order to have the complete computer-based parts operational, manual parts are also needed. Furthermore, there is a possibility that more or even all parts of an information system are manual.
Different types of manual operations are those which are:
M1: needed to effect personnel or material flows.
M2: impossible to formalise (e.g. decision making).
M3: susceptible to being formalised, but are manual by nature or an not be computer-based (e.g. economic reasons).
M4: manual support routines for a computer-based system.

The last three types are of importance in information systems development, M2 and M3 are dealt with during data system design (S3) and M4 during equipment adaptation (S4, see also figure 3.3.2). During this design step the manual routines with their relevant tasks are described and the requirements for the personnel to fulfil these tasks are analysed.
N.B. The ISAC-documentation gives an example of how to perform the S3-steps.

S.4. Equipment adaptation

Equipment adaption is divided into three steps:
- equipment study
- adaptation of computer-based routines
- creation of side routines

These steps are described chronologically, although as with previous study areas, iteration may be necessary.

S.4.1. Equipment study

During the data system design (S3) a suitable technology was chosen. Now the specific equipment per technology has to be decided upon. ISAC states that it is possible to wait until this phase, before making this choice of equipment.
The steps for the equipment study are:
- collection of facts and figures about equipment.
- identification of alternative equipment strategies.

- calculation of the size of the computer system.
- evaluation of equipment strategies.
- choice of suitable equipment.

Further details are given in the ISAC-literature.
The results of this study are documented in
<u>E-graphs</u> (equipment graphs).

S.4.2. Adaptation of computer-based routines

Adaptation (conversion etc.) routines are
designed similarly to the way in which programs
were designed in data system design (S3). These
routines transform physical data structures to
equipment independent structures or vice versa.
They are designed in two steps:
- design of physical data structures.
- design of adaptation routines.

The design of physical data structures is performed as follows:
1. Definition of methods for addresses and links;
   for datasets (files, etc.) using direct
   access, the address method has to be defined.
   If "records" have to be linked, the linking
   method must be defined.
2. Definition of record layouts for output,
   input, permanent and temporary datasets.
3. Allocation of secondary storage; for datasets
   on disk e.g. design decisions have to be taken
   regarding:
   - the allocation of datasets and programs on
     secondary units
   - the storage places for different datasets,
   - the size of overflow areas.
4. Determination of block sizes for records to be
   stored in blocks in order to optimise data
   processing.

The result of this design is documented in
<u>dataset,</u> <u>record</u> and <u>lay-out description</u>

The design of adaptation routines is needed
because differences occur between the physical
data structures and the equipment independent
('logical') data structures.
These routines provide the transformation between
the two structures.
They are designed as follows:
1. definition of error controls that check the
   input data for consistency and validity.

2. definition of adaptation routines for structure transformation (see above) and for error controls.
3 detailed design of adaptation routines done in the same way that programs were designed during data system design (S.3.2.).
4. supplementation of main programs with "open" and "close" operations (for those datasets that do not need adaptation routines).

S.4.3. Creation of support (side)routines

These routines are needed on the boundaries (interface) of a computer system to provide for input and output. They are designed like the manual parts (S.3.3.).
N.B. ISAC gives an example of the equipment adaptation phase.

.1.3. Documentation method

ISAC mentions a multitude of working procedure results that have to be documented. Here they are mentioned only briefly, with regard to content, organisation and techniques applied.

.1.3.1. Content
In the change analysis the following documentation is mentioned:

C.1: C.1.1. Problem table; example, no guidelines.
      C.1.2. Interest groups table; example, no guidelines.
      C.1.3. Problem groups table; example, no guidelines.
      C.1.4. Activity-model with A-graphs, text pages and property table. The technique is mentioned (see later). The level of detail is mentioned, not explicitly dealt with.
      C.1.5. Table of objectives; example, no guidelines.
      C.1.6. None.

C.2: C.2.1. Table of change aternatives; no guidelines.
      C.2.2. New A-model, new A-graph. (see C.1.4.).
      C.2.3. None.

C.3: C.3.1. Reason for choice; no guidelines.
      C.3.2. None.
      C.3.3. None.

In the problem oriented phase the following documentation is created:

S.1: S.1.1.   No guidelines are given as to the contents of the documentation required to describe the partitioning of an information system into multiple systems or sybsystems. The process of describing this partitioning by use of A-graphs is also not described. An example is given.
      S.1.1.1. Detailed A-graphs (see C.1.4.).
      S.1.1.2. Preliminary list of information systems; example, no content.

S.1.1.3. Classification of four types of
          information systems.
S.1.1.4. Delimitation of information sub-
          systems with regard to activities
          down to the level of output mes-
          sages with two aspects.
S.1.2.
S.1.2.1. Cost/benefit, benefits documented
          in property table.
S.1.2.2. Ambition levels in property table
          and in table of ambition levels
          (alternatives).
S.1.2.3. None.
S.1.2.4. Cost estimates description; no
          guidelines.
S.1.2.5. Choice of ambition level; no guide-
          lines.
S.1.3.
S.1.3.1. Relations of subsystems descrip-
          tion; no guidelines.
S.1.3.2. Priority rating; no guidelines.

S.2: S.2.1.   List of information sets; no guide-
              lines.
     S.2.1.1. Information analysis planning ta-
              ble; no guidelines for I-graphs
              (for technique see later).
     S.2.1.2. Precedence analysis, P-graph - I-
              graph (see technique).
     S.2.1.3. Component analysis, C-graph + term
              catalogue.
     S.2.2.
     S.2.2.1. Process list, names of information
              processes; example.
     S.2.2.2. Process tables (decision tables);
              example.
     S.2.3.   Property values in property tables
              (see S.1.2.1.).

In the <u>data oriented phase</u> the following documentation is created:

S.3: S.3.1.   Description of ways of processing,
              three levels; processing table with
              regard to the choice of ways of
              processing.
     S.3.2.   Data structure (logical). Program
              delimitation through D-graphs (see
              technique), lists of programs/-
              processes and dataset tables,

choice of data structures, program design according to Jackson structured programming methodology, P-graphs, control structures in D-structures, program structure in P-structures, data structure selection.

S.3.3.   Manual parts in M-graph.

S.4: S.4.1.   Description of equipment requirements in E-graph.

S.4.2.   Physical data structures in dataset and record layout descriptions.

S.4.3.   None.

N.B. In many cases the documentation is illustrated with examples.

102

.1.3.2. Techniques

ISAC uses as documentation techniques:
- A (activity)-graphs, text pages, property table (see figure 3.3.3.).
- I (information)-graphs (see figure 3.3.5.)
- C (component)-graphs (see figure 3.3.6.)
- D (data)-graphs.
- P (program)-structure.
- E (equipment)-graph.

N.B. Throughout the ISAC-description an example illustrates the different phases and steps, e.g. the transition from A-graph to I-graph etc. For data and program structuring the Jackson Structured Programming methodology is used.

.1.3.3. Organisation

The organisation of the documentation is not explained in the ISAC-description. Neither are documentation tools mentioned. A coding system is given as an example. The topic of support by means of a project secretariat is not handled.

.1.4. Project management method

ISAC mentions project administration, encompassing project organisation, project planning and project follow-up.
The ISAC-group feels that "project administration" approaches can be seen as tools for the information system development project and that the ISAC-methodology can be applied in conjunction with several project management methods. Further explanation however is not given, although it is pointed out that these methods must be able to operate in harmony with the technique of change analysis and with the philosophy of learning through communication, which is one of the basic ISAC principles.

.2. <u>Evaluation-matrix ISAC.</u>

| | | philosophy | working procedure | documentation method | | | project-management method |
				tech	org	cont	
Company analysis/ synthesis	1.1						
	1.2						
	1.3						
project-selection							
Logical design	3.1	▨	▨	▨		▨	
	3.2						
Logical → technical	4.1	▨	▨	▨		▨	
	4.2						
Technical design	5.1	▨	▨	▨		▨	
	5.2						
Physical design	6.1						
	6.2	▨	▨	▨		▨	
	6.3						
	6.4						
implementation							
exploitation							

.3 Applicability of the methodology

.3.1. Description of the matrix coverage

.3.1.1. Corporate analysis/-synthesis

The ISAC methodology can be used for corporate analysis and synthesis. Although it is not particularly meant for this phase, it should indeed be possible to 'list' problems and identify interest groups on a company-wide basis.
The description can be made by means of a broad activity-graph using SDA-techniques. The analysis of company goals can be performed as well as the evaluation of the present situation and proposals for improvements.

In the ISAC description which was studied, no rules for precise definition of activities, or for recognising activities in practice, were given. Until formal definitions are provided, an activity at this level may be described as a main process and/or a process (see chapter 2 and appendix 2).

- The ISAC methodology can thus be applied for an integral company analysis/synthesis. The overall process structure must then consist of an overall activity graph.

- The integral analysis/synthesis of data and data structures is not dealt with.

- The description of a company model in conjunction with an information/automation plan is not mentioned in ISAC.
  However, it must be recognized that a number of activities in the change analysis point in this direction.

.3.1.2. Project selection

Change analysis mentions the choice of a change strategy which includes the selection of 'problem groups'. This means that a project selection as described in chapter 2 should be possible. Such a project selection process should also be aided by ISAC's inclusion of a cost/benefit analysis which covers human, social and economic aspects.
However, ISAC does not explicitly mention the project selection process.

.3.1.3. Logical design

This phase is covered by ISAC's problem oriented analysis in conjunction with the activity study and the information analysis. ISAC has recognized the importance of this phase and the two subsequent phases (the logical-to-technical phase and the technical phase itself) in two ways:
- the notation of the A-graph, I-graph and C-graph is useful for all three phases.
- sufficient practical level of detail is given for each step e.g. the precedence and component analysis, and the 'process analysis'.

A critical requirement of this phase is the ability to identify the information subsystems upon which the activity study and information analysis are based. The ISAC approach is similar to that outlined in chapter 2 of this report, although ISAC obviously uses a different terminology.

Activities (or processes) are described in a top-down manner starting from change analysis. In the subsequent phase of activity analysis, the relationships between the activities and the data are explained by means of techniques such as precedence and component analysis, I-graphs and, finally, D-graphs. These activity-to-data relationships are performed in an interactive, iterative way (see chapter 2).
It is regrettable, however, that no definitions are given for terms such as: "information (sub)-system," "activity", "process" etc. and that no guidelines are given as to how to recognise these "entities" in practice. The use of the terms is illustrated by means of an example i.e. the study of a company.

.3.1.4. Transformation

In the last chapter of the ISAC documentation studied (1), the relations between the activities in the different phases, and in particular the outputs of these, are summarised. The transformation from logical design (problem oriented) to technical design (data oriented) activities takes place with the aid of the transition from A-grpahs to I-graphs and to D-graphs.
The I- and C-graphs with the (information) process tables are derived from precedence and component analysis, and are used to build the D-

106

and P-structures and, finally, the E-graphs.
The transformation as described in chapter 2
appears to be feasible for both the process and
data oriented components of the project cycle.
The connection of ISAC to the Jackson Structured
Programming methodology appears to be less well
established.

.3.1.5. Technical design
In ISAC terms this phase could be called 'data
system design'. In this phase ISAC constructs D-
graphs, D-structures as well as P-structures,
which are based on the previously built A-, I-
and C-graphs.
An E-graph which is independent of any equipment
(configuration) considerations is also constructed. This graph includes the types of
processing required for the manual parts of the
information system. D-graphs and D-structures are
used to handle the data-side of technical design,
and P-structures are used to handle the process-
side. The synthesis mentioned in chapter 2 is
achieved by means of E-graphs.

.3.1.6. Physical design
Programs: For the setting up of the program
               structures, ISAC refers to the
               Jackson Structured Programming metho-
               dology (JSP). How the actual pro-
               gramming should be performed is not
               detailed.

User proce-   for the design of the user procedures
dures   ISAC mentions four steps and illus-
               trates them by means of an example.
               It is felt that far more attention
               should be paid to this part of the
               design work.

EDP centre   ISAC does not deal with this explic-
procedure.   itly.

File   for construction of the data structu-
design   res, including the physical structu-
               res, ISAC refers to the JSP methodo-
               logy.
               It should be pointed out that the JSP
               methodology is meant, in principle,
               for logical data structures design,
               not for the physical construction of

files. The actual construction, e.g. in the sense of DBA activities, is not given.

.3.1.7. Implementation

The implementation of the automated information system, as the product of the project activities, is not dealt with in ISAC as such. ISAC does state that user involvement is essential in the implementation phase if it is to be carried out smoothly.

.3.1.8 Operation

Operational aspects of the system, including maintenance and evaluation are not dealt with by ISAC.

.3.2. Thoroughness of the methodology

The change analysis (corporate analysis/synthesis), the problem oriented work, such as activity analysis and information analysis, as well as the data oriented work, such as data system design and equipment adaptation, are described in great detail in the ISAC methodology.

Although not all definitions of terms are equally applicable or useable, the examples given in the ISAC literature go a long way towards making up this deficiency.

.3.3. Row transition

In those aspects of corporate analysis/synthesis which are covered by ISAC, the emphasis is on the process side (see chapter 2) with the use of the activity study techniques.

Global analysis/synthesis of data and data structures is not recognized in this phase. The overall activities graph can be seen as the 'corporate model'.

Connection to the next phase of project selection is possible by use of techniques such as the cost/effectiveness study, priority allocation and interest group definition. These, and other, ISAC techniques make it possible to choose between the alternatives outlined in change analysis.

The generalised activity graphs and supporting documentation are used to make the transition to the logical design. Both process analysis and data analysis are now carried out, athough ISAC does not use these exact terms.

The transformation from logical to technical

machine independent design is also supported by ISAC. One of the tools used to achieve this transformation is the SDA notation technique. ISAC handles this transition well, especially since it emphasises that equipment adaptation is performed at a later stage. This means that the resulting technical design is as independent as possible of the final technical equipment chosen for the implementation.

The transition to the physical design is possible with regard to the documentation method column, but ISAC refers to the application of the JSP methodology to cover other transition needs in this phase. This means that ISAC itself cannot be said to cover all of the physical design rows.

ISAC does not cover the subsequent phases.

.3.4. Column coordination

The ISAC philosophy is, in essence, based upon a tripartite approach that deals with processes (activities), data, and organisation units (interest groups). Starting from this philosophy it is felt that the transition to the working procedure is implicitly described, especially as far as the change analysis and the problem oriented work are concerned. The documentation method is integrated with the working procedure in such a way that the documentation is created rather smoothly throughout the whole development cycle. Only the organisation of the documentation is missing here.

This is partly due to the absence of a project management method for which ISAC refers to existing methods.

.4. Observations

The ISAC methodology covers a great deal of the evaluation matrix. However, the methodology should be more explicit about the overall data (information) analysis/syntheses and the project selection within the first phases, including the construction and use of a 'company model'.

The physical design has to be extended so as to provide guidelines for the programming, the design of procedures for the computer centre, and the file construction. Though the ISAC team actually used the Jackson Structured Programming methodology in 1976, it is felt that a question

remains as to whether or not this methodology can be integrated as smoothly as suggested.
Furthermore, it is felt that ISAC lacks the working procedure to synthesize the process related D-structures into a logical overall data (information) model.

The implementation and operation phases should also be covered within the ISAC methodology.
ISAC lacks tools for the organisation and support of the documentation method. Support tools, other than notation techniques, are not supplied. Possibly PSL/PSA (see 3.10) can provide a solution here, although this possibility needs to be studied in more detail.

ISAC has, as yet, provided no project management method. The question to be answered here is whether or not the ISAC working procedure, which has its own phasing and grouping of actions, can be directly related to the procedural steps of existing project management methodologies such as SDM, PRODOSTA, PROMPT or AFA.
Finally, it should be pointed out that the Delta Lloyd insurance group in the Netherlands have combined ISAC with the Data Analysis techniques of CACI, UK. This appears to have been done to make up for the lack of integral data analysis tools in the first phase of ISAC.
In conclusion, it can be stated that the ISAC methodology is one of the most complete methodologies studied by the evaluation team. Perhaps this accounts for the formation of the Dutch ISAC users group (3).

References

(1) Lundeberg, M. et al   - "A Systematic Approach to Information Systems Development".
Part I and II.
University of Stockholm, Department of Information Systems, Stockholm, May 1978.

(2)   - "The Analysis of User Needs".
EDP-Analyzer, January 1979, Vol 17 no. 1.

(3) Ruys, H.P.   - "De ISAC-methode".
Informatie, Vol 23, no. 5, Amsterdam, May 1981.

(4) Lundeberg, M. et al   Information Systems Development, a systematic approach.
Prentice-Hall Inc.,1981 Englewood Cliffs, N.J.

(5) Lundeberg, M. et al   De ISAC-methodiek
Samson, Alphen a/d Rijn 1981

3.4. Description of the MOS-method.

.1.   Outline of the methodology.

.1.1. Philosophy.

The MOS-method (Methodical Design of Systems) is
an interconnected set of techniques derived
(mainly) from the results of the ISAC-project (1)
and from the Entity-Attribute-Relations model of
Codasyl (2).
The ISAC project extended the information theory
of Prof. Langefors into a practical form. The
resulting systems analysis and design approach
has attained a broad following in Europe.
The ISAC-results have been integrated with concepts from the Codasyl entity-attribute-relationship model (2) and the normalization approach of
Codd (3) by employees of Desisco Ltd. (4) and
were incorporated into a systems design course.
The philosophy contains the following elements:
- obtain a thorough understanding of the present
  situation, bottle-necks and desires for improvement using ISAC change-analysis and activity-study concepts.
  Change-analysis is the analysis and description of the present situation, the problems
  and desires by use of precedence-graphs and
  entity relationship models, and the determination and evaluation of alternative solutions.
  The selected solution (the new situation) is
  in the form of a precedence-graph and is the
  basis for the precedence-analysis method. (see
  figure 3.4.1).
  A precedence-graph relates outputs and inputs
  to the sub-systems that can be recognized in
  the problem-area.
  During the activity-study both information and
  material flows and processes are considered. A
  hierarchical top-down decomposition takes
  place, starting with a decomposition of the
  outputs and working backwards towards the
  accordingly decomposed inputs of the
  precedence-graph.

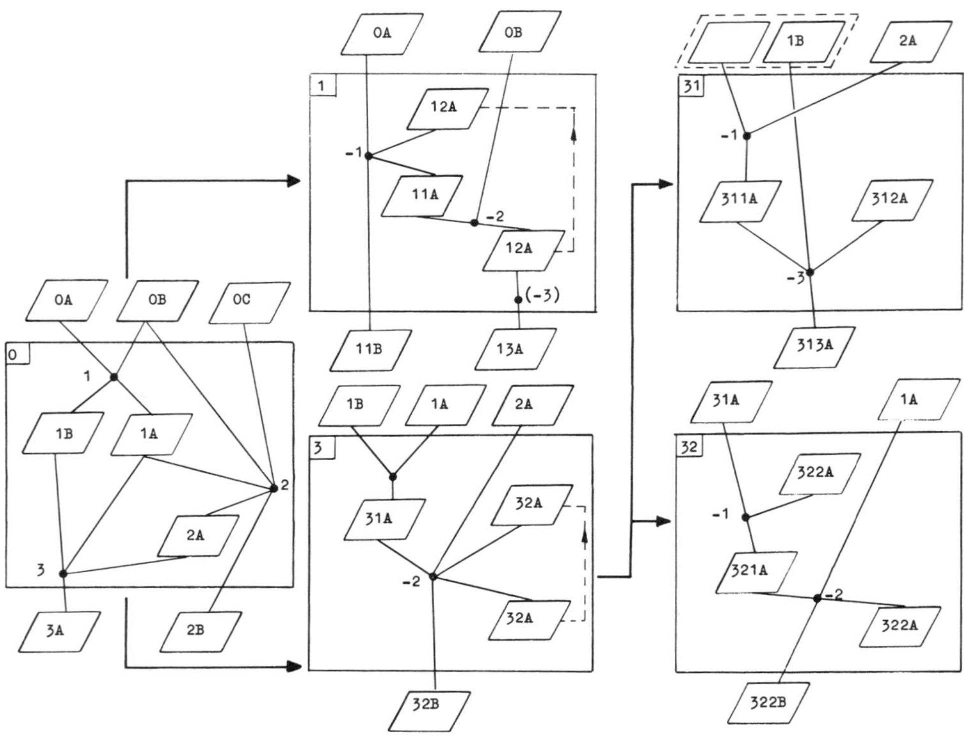

Figure 3.4.1 An example of a precedence graph
hierarchy.

- During the decomposition process the information-sets are analysed for the presence of
  objects, which are then used to build an
  entity-relationship-model; this model in turn
  influences the decomposition process. This
  interaction between precedence-analysis-
  decomposition and data-modelling is maintained
  throughout the logical and technical design.
  Apart from this, coupling and binding rules
  (5) are used to aid decomposition and synthesis.
- Process-specification takes place at the
  lowest level of detail. At every precedence-
  level, however, a complete definition of
  objects and processes takes place, accurately
  defining the objects for everyone concerned.
  Aspects of interest are recorded in aspect-
  tables.

- The user-oriented approach of ISAC is followed: where possible, user-participation is
  encouraged. The precedence-graphs are the main
  intermediary to ensure understanding between
  the parties involved.

.1.2. Working procedures.

An overview of the MOS-methodology is depicted in
figure 3.4.2.

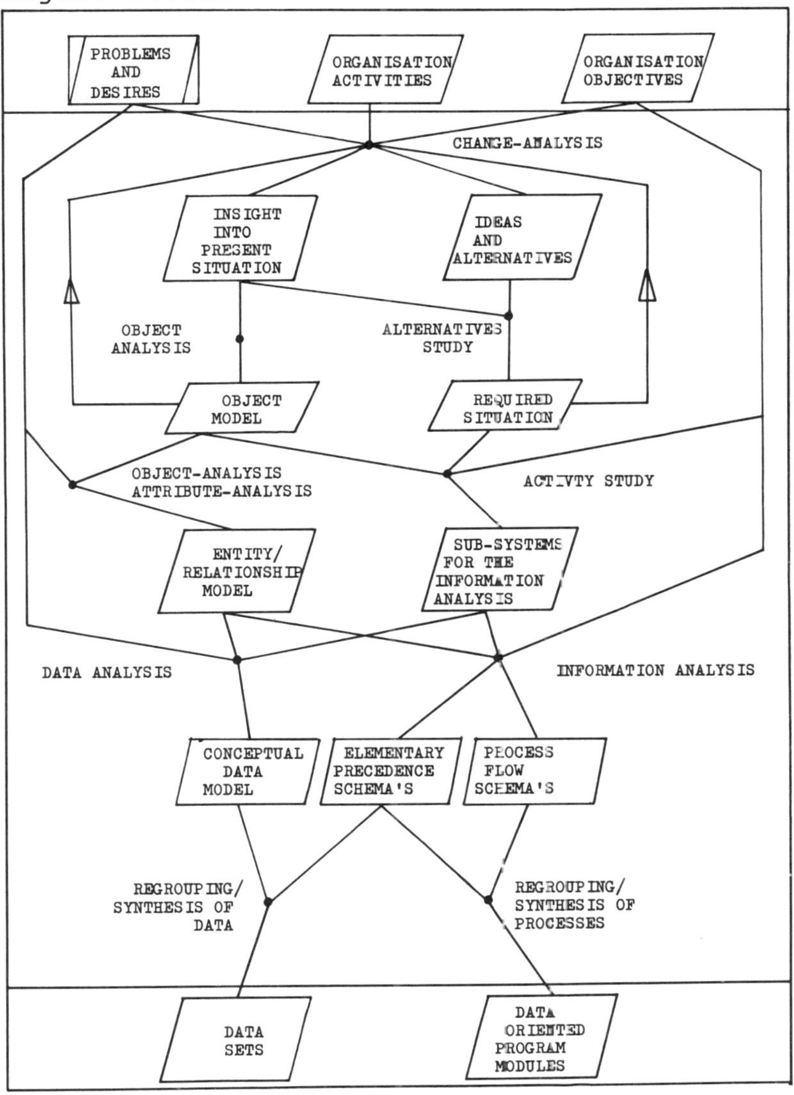

Figure 3.4.2 An overview of MOS.

114

.1.2.1 ISAC change-analysis is used to obtain an
insight into the present situation , the
problems, desires for change and the
objectives of the organisation in the area
under consideration. This leads to ideas
and alternatives for improvement.
Precedence-graphs are made of the present
situation and of the alternative solutions.

.1.2.2 Object-analysis leads to an entity-relationship model of the objects so far recognised.

.1.2.3 Activity-study takes the precedence-schema
of the selected problem-solution as a
basis for the top-down precedence-analysis
decomposition method.

.1.2.4 Results of the activity-study are used in
an iterative way for extending the data-
model. Conversely the data-model is used
for the decomposition process. This interaction is continued throughout the method.
Also coupling and binding principles are
used. Conclusion of the activity-study is
reached when recognizable and completely
defined sub-systems are reached.

.1.2.5 Information-analysis is a series of iterative techniques consisting of component-
analysis (decomposition of the information
sets), precedence-analysis and process-
analysis.
Results from the component-analysis are
used in parallel for the data-analysis,
which leads to an entity- attribute relationship model of the problem-area.
The data-model conversely is used to give
criteria for the decomposition-process:
decomposition of the outputs of a precedence-schema follows as much as possible
the (normalised) objects of the data-
model.
Results are:
 . precedence-graphs at an elementary level
   (i.e. the information-sets are decomposed to a sufficient level of detail to
   be able to design the automated, data-
   oriented system).

- a normalised data-model (conceptual data model)
- process-flow schema's showing per sub-system the flows of elementary messages starting from the initial inputs and showing the flows between the elementary processes and the flows crossing the low-level precedence-schema boundaries until they leave the system boundaries. (figure 3.4.3)

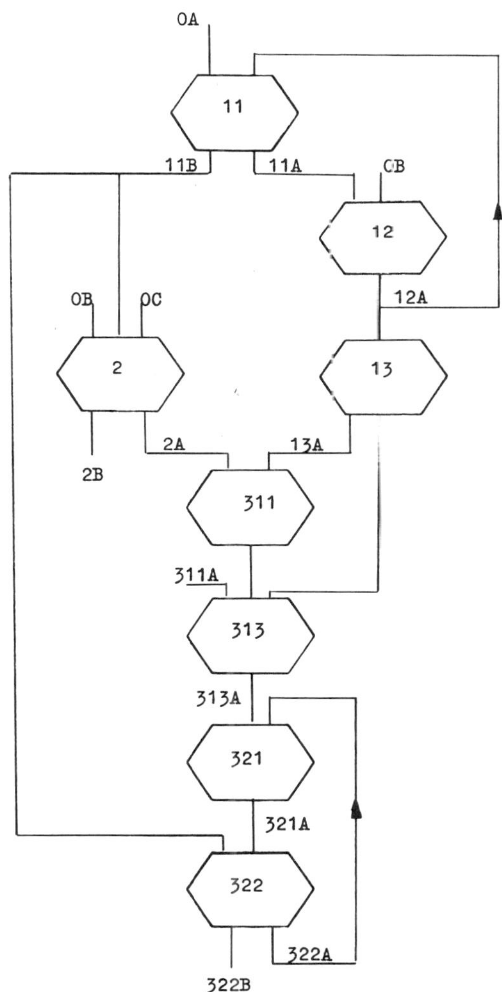

Figure 3.4.3 Process-flow schema.

- Various matrices showing the relationships between processes, information sets, data and work-stations.

116

.1.2.6 Synthesis and regrouping of information
processes and information sets takes
place, using so-called incidence-matrices
(for regrouping and completeness-checking)
and the results from previous phases.
Regrouping and synthesis of information-
sets is done on the basis of information-
set types (external, cyclic, frequency-
bridging and man-readable information-
sets) and in such a way that the conceptual data-model is reflected as much as
possible. (Entity-directed approach).
Regrouping and synthesis of elementary
processes is based on process-types, frequencies, place of execution, etc. and is
done in such a way that, in so far as it
is possible, incoming objects are handled
by one process only. The process-flow
schema and the data-set-process matrix are
used as a basis.

.1.2.7 Machine-independent design is completed by
choosing the file-design, establishing I/O
modules and specifying programs in such a
way, that the results can be used in a
structured program-design method like
Michael Jackson's (6).

<u>.1.3. Documentation-method.</u>

Most of the methods and techniques employed make
use of the documentation results from previous
steps.
Change analysis and alternatives study lead to
the first precedence-graph, which is decomposed
by the same technique throughout the levels of
activity-study and information-analysis. The
object model is transformed into the conceptual
data-model in successive iterations during
object-, attribute- and data-analysis.
The lowest level precedence-graphs are used for
making the structure-schemas, which are a basis
for the program-module and file-structure design.

.1.4. Project-Management Method.

The MOS-method is not embedded in a project-management method. The Desisco-team is working on a project life-cycle for MOS. This life-cycle will allow for connections with most of the phase-oriented project management methods as e.g. the Prodosta method (7). The availability of such a connection will be a help, because there are no formalised milestones in the method.
The conclusion of the activity-study and information-analysis phases both depend on the requirements of the problem-area, such as the complexity, the diversity of the span of control and the size.
This decision is for the larger part left to the experience and insight of the designer.
Linking up with a project-management method will require the formalisation of milestones in the method, as is done in e.g. SASO (8).

.2. <u>Evaluation-matrix MOS.</u>

		philosophy	working procedure	documentation method			project-management method
				tech	org	cont	
Company analysis/ synthesis	1.1						
	1.2						
	1.3						
project-selection							
Logical design	3.1	/////	/////	/////	/////	/////	
	3.2	/////	/////	/////	/////	/////	
Logical → technical	4.1	/////	/////	/////	/////	/////	
	4.2	/////	/////	/////	/////	/////	
Technical design	5.1	/////	/////	/////	/////	/////	
	5.2	/////	/////	/////	/////	/////	
Physical design	6.1						
	6.2						
	6.3						
	6.4						
implementation							
exploitation							

.3. Applicability of the methodology.

.3.1 Description of the matrix-coverage.

As has been shown in paragraph 2, the method covers the area of logical and technical design. The method gives no connection with a method for the determination of the information/automation plan. By extending the area under consideration to the whole of the organisation it would be possible to obtain an activity-model and entity-relationship model of the organisation, but the tools are not designed for such an approach and different techniques would be needed to make this possible.
The logical and technical design phases are reasonably covered.
Formalisation of the end-points of activity-study and information analysis would be a help to the average designteam.
The interaction of datamodelling, information modelling and the use of the normalised datamodel as decomposition and synthesis tools during the logical design-phase seems an excellent approach. It makes the technical design phase simpler and allows for consistency of naming-conventions. This latter point is especially important for Data-Dictionary/Directory usage and for the automated support of the design-process (which is not supplied by MOS, however.).
Data- and information-structuring is the best worked-out part of the method.
Process-analysis is not formalised and consists mainly of check-lists. Decision-tables are mentioned as a possible tool and described as part of the design-course.
Dialogue and DB/DC design are not a formalised part of the method. The data-process interaction basis of the method leads naturally to a structured programming approach such as Michael Jackson's.

.3.2. Thoroughness of the methodology.

Desisco is working on a project-management connection. As long as this connection is not available, a problem may arise from the fact that there is a very strict separation between logical and physical design in MOS: technical aspects are

deferred until after the logical design.
Nevertheless, from project management demands,
the need arises to analyse technical aspects in
early stages, e.g. for cost/benefit analysis and
the purchasing of hardware.
The interaction between datamodelling and function modelling gives an early insight in the
overall datamodel and may permit an early division into sub-systems for detailed and separate
analysis. This may help in simplifying the technical specification per sub-system and in redu-
cing lead-times for the technical design phase.

.3.3. Row transition.

The connections between the steps in the logical
and technical design phase are in general well-
coordinated. The method takes the designer in
well defined steps through the analysis and
design processes.
A better formalisation of the process-design
phase is required and extensions towards dialogue
and DB/DC design are desirable.

.3.4. Column coordination.

Translation from philosophy to working-procedures
(excluding dialogue and DB/DC design) has been
excellently and consequentially done.
MOS does not include an automated documentation
and developmentsupport tool, which we feel is
essential for a structured, top-down approach,
due to the large amount of detail that must be
handled at the lowest levels of decomposition. It
might be possible to link MOS to, for example,
PSL/PSA (9).

.4. Observations.

MOS is more than a technique, it is also a philosophy that must be used as a permanent background
reference when using the MOS-techniques in practice. This requires that a good course be available and that coaching of the method in practice
can be supplied.
Both are provided by Desisco Ltd. The documentation of the course could do with a new release

to bring it up-to-date with the latest status of
the method.

References.

1) M. Lundeberg.   A systematic approach to
                         Information-systems
                         Development, part I and
                         II, Univ. of Stockholm,
                         May 1978.

2)   ISO-TC97/SC5/WG3.
                         Concepts and Terminology
                         for the conceptual
                         schema and the Informa-
                         tion Base, March 1982

3) Codd, E.F.   Normalized   Data-Base
                         Structure: A brief Tuto-
                         rial. Proceedings of the
                         1971 ACM Sigfidet Work-
                         shop on Data Description
                         and Access.

4)   MOS - Systems Analysis
                         and   Technical   Design
                         Course parts I and II,
                         1979.

5) E.Yourdon,   Structured Design 1978.
   L.L. Constantine

6) M.Jackson Systems Ltd -JSD Tutorial, 1981

7) P.Boosman   Prodosta Users Package.
   W.J.P.E.v.d.Bragt   IDM/AP/77-97134,   June
                         1977,   Cat.nr.   770046
                         (Philips)

8)   Description of the SASO-
                         method. Chapter 3.5 of
                         this publication.

9) A.H.J.B.Schotgerrits Het   ISDOS projekt en
    H. Gersteling.   PSL/PSA. Informatie,
                         sept. 1981.(in Dutch)

10)Codd, E.F.   Further Normalization of
                         the Data-Base Relational
                         Model.   IBM   Research
                         Laboratory, San Jose,
                         (August 1971) R.J.909.

3.5. <u>SASO</u>

.1. <u>Outline of the methodology</u>

.1.1. <u>Philosophy</u>

The SASO-method (Systems Analysis Systems Design method) is a series of interconnected techniques brought together by the brothers A. and P.- Blokdijk, continually proved in a practical environment and formalized into courses by IBM-Netherlands (1).

It covers the logical and technical design phases of an automated information system and, partly, the physical design phase. The method is based on the ideas of Professor Langefors, which were extended and translated into a practical form by M.Lundeberg c.s. as part of the ISAC-project (2). The resulting information theory has attained a broad following in Europe.

This basis has been improved upon and has been extended with methods and techniques from various sources and has been welded together in a consistent and complete whole by the Blokdijks.

The philosophy contains the following elements:

  -the starting point of the formalized method is a description of the object system and the (new) information system to support this, in the form of a so-called precedence-graph. (see figure 3.5.1).

  The existing system and organisation are not explicitly studied and described, and are only used as a means to get an understanding of the area under analysis.

  As such SASO is an agent which facilitates change.

  -The precedence-graph relates output and input (both information and material flows) with the sub-systems that can be recognised and which reflect the new, required situation.

  A hierarchical top-down decomposition takes place, starting from this so-called O-graph, using the method of precedence-analysis i.e. for each sub-system of the O-graph a new precedence-graph is drawn, showing a decomposition of the outputs, the required processes and (working-back towards) the inputs.

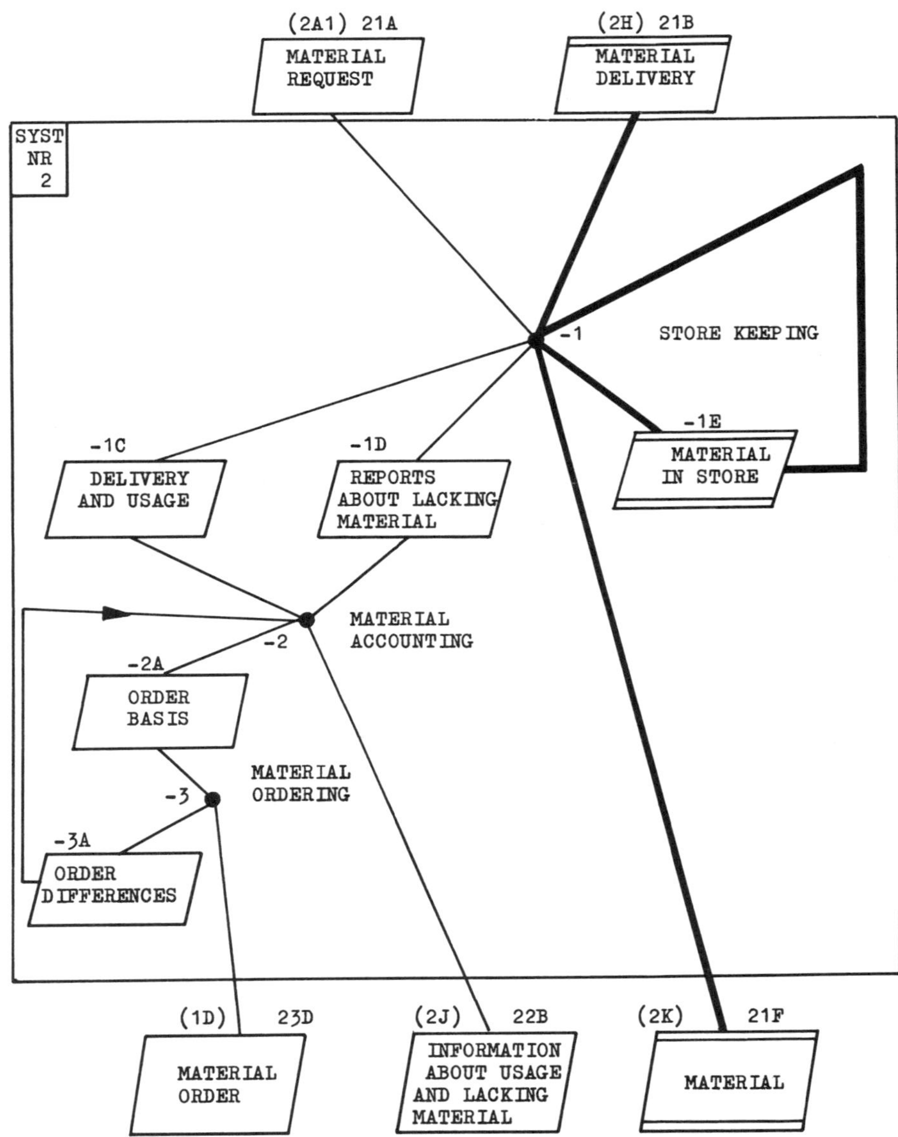

Figure 3.5.1: A SASO precedence-graph of the
2nd level.

-This decomposition process continues down to
two levels:
a.the level of the so-called independent procedure, i.e. a procedure which, when trig-

gered, proceeds to its logical conclusion without needing information from other sources, other than the information available at the start. In other words, it is a time-independent and uninterrupted procedure. The independent procedure has a limited complexity in terms of "binding-rules", described a.o. by Yourdon and Constantine (3). This phase is called object-systems analysis and design.

  b.the level of the "elementary-message" which consists in its simplest form of an identifier, an attribute and if necessary a time-constraint.

This decomposition phase is called information analysis.

-Process-specification takes place at the lowest level of detail and after the conceptual data-(base) schema has been determined for the entire area under analysis.

-Data specification takes place after the information analysis has been completed to its most detailed level. Data-analysis on a more global level, e.g. on the Entity-Relations level is not part of the SASO-method.

-Active user participation in the phases up to, and including, object system analysis and during terminal-dialogue design, is an essential part of the method.

.1.2. Working procedure.

The SASO-methodology consist of the following methods and techniques, to be applied in the various phases of an automation project. (See also figure 3.5.2).

The figure shows at the top-line the results that are reached during the phases that are mentioned at the bottom-line.

The body shows how the problem area under consideration after the objectives analysis and systemboundary determination is decomposed into a number of subsystems during object-system design, until via a number of decomposition levels the level of the independent procedure is reached.

During information analysis, component analysis and data-analysis, each independent procedure is further analysed and decomposed.

An overall control and normalisation activity then leads to a conceptual data-base model after which each independent procedure is further

analysed during the process-analysis and
dialogue- or batch-design and user procedure
phases. Eventually this leads to the technical
and physical design-phases, which are not shown
in detail.
The SASO-methodology consists of the following
methods and techniques which are applied in the
phases mentioned in figure 3.5.2:

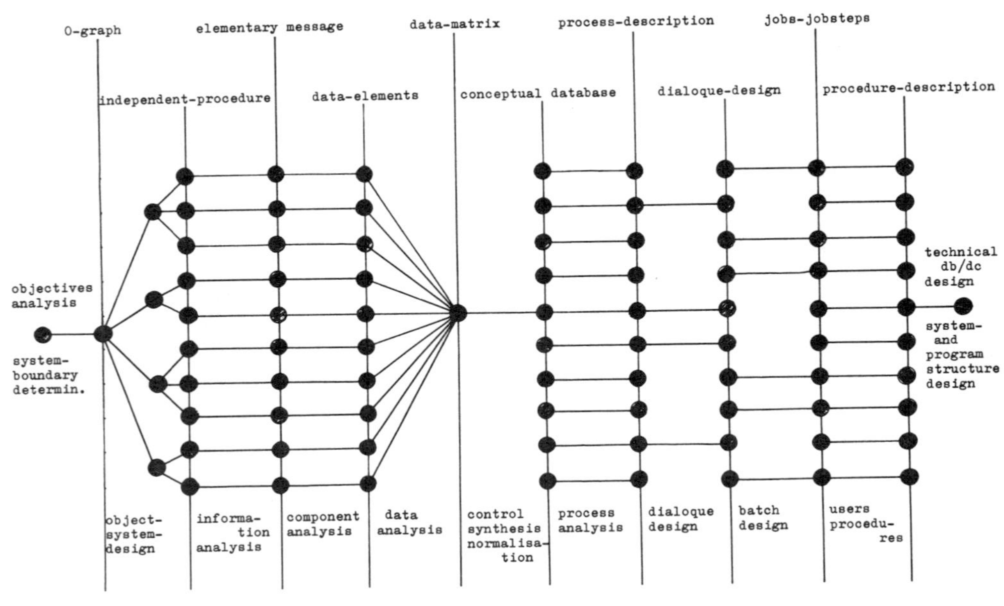

Figure 3.5.2   SASO methods and techniques.

.1.2.1. Objectives analysis.
This technique is applied to establish the
weights of the various objectives and the possible alternatives for the system design. The
method of weighted ranking used as shown in the
example of figure 1.2.

.1.2.2. Determination of the system boundary.
The boundary of the system is determined by
specifying the inputs and outputs of the first
precedence graph (the O-graph).
A formalised way for this determination e.g. by
means of an information model of the firm is not
part of the method.

Parts of the Business Systems Planning (BSP) method of IBM are being tried out as an upwards extension to SASO.
Also a formalised group interview method (Metaplan) is being used to obtain a better insight into the problems, bottle-necks and wishes experienced by personnel in the area under study.
This helps in determining priorities, functions to be included and attitudes of people involved.
It also gives an indication as to the type of user-members to be included in the project team.

.1.2.3. <u>Object system analysis.</u>
This is the analysis of the interaction between the object system and the supporting information system, using the technique of precedence analysis and a top-down decomposition approach. With the help of coupling and binding principles (3), structuring criteria for the new system are established.

.1.2.4. <u>Alternatives determination and evaluation</u>
Supported by the results of the object system analysis and objectives determination, various alternatives are put forward and evaluated.
This process is made easier by the decomposition into independent procedures. The internal functioning of each procedure can then be studied independently of its relationships to other procedures. Their relationship can, in turn, be studied via dynamic interactions and information flows between the procedures.

.1.2.5. <u>Information system analysis.</u>
Starting from the results of the object system analysis, the precedence analysis decomposition technique is continued to the level of the elementary message and elementary process. At this level a detailed description of the data flow and the hierarchical structure of the data can be produced.

.1.2.6. <u>Component analysis and data analysis.</u>
The result of these activities is a description of the elementary messages and the data elements they consist of. An analysis is made also of the activities performed by the various processes on these data elements e.g.: is there a process which generates, deletes, updates and uses the various data elements.

This is documented in the form of tables and matrices.
This phase is, in fact, a thorough check on the completeness and consistency of the systems model derived so far.

.1.2.7. Derivation of the conceptual data model.

The bubble charting method of Date is used to establish the normalised data model of Codd. It leads to an entity-attribute-relationship model, which will be the basis for the technical data-base design.
Because of the interaction between processes and data, especially in the on-line sphere, the first phase of the dialogue design, giving an insight into the data usage, is done in parallel with this step.

.1.2.8. Process analysis.

This is performed using Nassi-Shneidermann diagrams and decision tables.
It is based on the documentation produced during information analysis and data and component analysis. The conceptual data-base design is also used.

.1.2.9. Dialogue Design.

With the use of HIPO-like Finite State Diagrams, the interaction between users, terminal and computer is described. Particular attention is given to the overall control structure.
The screen layouts are established with the active participation of the end-user.
For this phase standard screen building and simulation aids are available within IBM such as IIAS and IIPS.

.1.2.10. User-Procedures.

These can be described with the precedence techniques already described or with the HIPO-technique of IBM.

.1.2.11. Technical Data-Base Design.

Starting from the conceptual data-base design and the process- and dialogue descriptions, the technical DL/I-DB design is derived in a number of formalised steps.
DB-prototype (an IBM-product) can be used to check alternative solutions.

.1.2.12. <u>Technical DC-design.</u>
This consists of the preparation of design specifications for the Message Formatting Services (a technical description of the screens and the connections between them), calculation of resource usage, specification of technical requirements and security needs.

.1.2.13. <u>System and program Structure.</u>
Design of the system and program structure is done according to the Jackson principles.
It is based on the technical data-base design, the DB/DC design, and the process analysis.

.1.3. <u>Documentation method.</u>
Most of the methods and techniques used within SASO make excellent use of the documentation, i.e. documentation results automatically from the technique used and this is then the basis for the next step.
The system boundary determination leads to the first (highest level) precedence graph of the object system analysis.
Object system analysis and Information analysis use the same precedence technique which is followed at the lowest level by the decomposition of the elementary messages into data elements.
These results are used to build the data tables and matrices during the component and data analysis.
The bubble-charting method of Date (6) gives documentation about the data-structures as a product of normalisation.
The Nassi-Shneidermann diagrams and Decision Tables used in Process Analysis serve as the documentation for this activity. The same applies to the HIPO-like diagrams of the dialogue design.
No formalised, structured documentation is produced during the objectives analysis or the alternatives determination and evaluation

.1.4. <u>Project Management Method.</u>
The SASO method is not embedded in a formal project management method.
There are a number of milestones in SASO which can be used as anchor points for the project management interface.
These are:
   -the O-graph, at which point the boundaries of

the problem area and the subsystems are sharp-
ly defined by the incoming and outgoing information and material flows.
-the end of the object system description, at
which point the independent procedures and the
information and material flows as well as the
dynamic aspects of the system (triggers, frequencies, conditions and constraints) are
known.
-the level of the conceptual data-base design,
at which point the conceptual data model and
the use of the data elements by the elementary
processes, are known. At this point also the
decisions about sequential and parallel development of the sub-systems can be made.
It is, however, left to the user to work out the
details of the projectmanagement interface.

.2. <u>Evaluation-matrix SASO.</u>

| | | philosophy | working procedure | documentation method | | | project-management method |
				tech	org	cont	
Company analysis/ synthesis	1.1						
	1.2						
	1.3						
project-selection							
Logical design	3.1	/////	/////	/////	/////	/////	
	3.2	/////	/////	/////	/////	/////	
Logical → technical	4.1	/////	/////	/////	/////	/////	
	4.2	/////	/////	/////	/////	/////	
Technical design	5.1	/////	/////	/////	/////	/////	
	5.2	/////	/////	/////	/////	/////	
Physical design	6.1	/////	/////	/////	/////	/////	
	6.2						
	6.3						
	6.4	/////	/////	/////	/////	/////	
implementation							
exploitation							

132

.3   Applicability of the methodology.

.3.1   Description of the matrix coverage.
As shown in the evaluation matrix, the method covers the area of the logical and technical design
and partly that of the physical design. The method provides no connection to the information-
/automation plan.
By extending the problem area under consideration
to the whole of the company, the technique of
objectives analysis can help in project selection.
BSP-like techniques have been tried out in SASO,
but have not yet been officially incorporated in
the method.
The logical design phase, especially the activities starting from the O-graph up to and including the design of the conceptual data-base
model, the process-analysis and the dialogue
design form a reasonably complete and consistent
method, leading via formalised steps to the
required end results. In the technical design
phase, the technical data-base and the batch-
system design leading via the Jackson approach to
the program design seems to be fairly complete.
The DC-design needs a little more body. Also the
first phases of the method leading to the object
system analysis could do with extensions in the
direction of value-engineering, change-analysis
and the formulation of a global data model e.g.
on an entity relationship basis, to be followed
by e.g. Bubble-Charting or Normalisation steps.

.3.2   Thoroughness of the methodology.
In many project management systems, the logical
design phase covers the phases of the feasibility
study and logical design,
the main difference being the level of penetra-
tion into the area under analysis.
As pointed out in paragraph 1.4 there are a number of milestones at which these project-management interfaces can be made:
  - -the level of the O-graph for the start of the
     feasibility study.
  - -the end of the object system description for
     the start of the logical design.

A problem can arise from the fact that there is a
very strict separation between logical and physical design in SASO: technical aspects are defer-

red until after the logical design.
Nevertheless, from project management demands the
need arises to analyse technical aspects in early
stages, e.g. for cost/ benefit analysis and the
purchasing of hardware.
We feel however that SASO, through its independent procedure approach, gives a better basis for
these cost benefit analysis steps, than when a
less formalised approach is used.
Very good results can be expected when practice
has established norms for the amount of effort
that needs to be spent on the analysis and development of these independent procedures.
The third milestone mentioned, the level of the
conceptual data-base design, could be incorporated as an extra decision point in the project
phasing.
As this point the impact of the various subsystems on the data usage, and the interaction
between sub-systems, are clearly defined. The
order in which systems development can take place
is also known. It is, in effect, an excellent "go
or no-go" point, except for the fact that it
occurs rather late in the cycle.
The reason that this point is so late in the analysis phase, is that it requires an integrated
data-model which covers the whole area under analysis.
Our suggestion is to determine a global model at
an earlier stage e.g. by means of an entity-relationship approach, this milestone could be moved
to an earlier point in the cycle.

.3.3 Row transition.
As discussed above, the connections between steps
over the whole area covered are very well coordinated. The method takes the analyst in well-defi-
ned steps from result to result to the end result
as defined by the method.
Extensions upwards in the direction of BSP-like
techniques are still under consideration.
Also the methods of Thunnissen (CVI) using cyber-
netical principles and information-value determination could be profitably explored.

.3.4 Column coordination.
The translation from philosophy to working procedures is excellent. Only the extension of the
binding theory to working procedures has not been
done. This has been left in the form of hints for

the analyst.
Also naming conventions, especially necessary for
the recognition, definition and interpretation of
the large volume of data elements, keys, etc. are
painfully missed.
The ideas incorporated in 'Charade' are being
tried-out as a solution. Also the "role-concept"
of Nyssen (10) could be a help.
SASO does not include a tool for an automated
documentation and development support.We feel
such a tool is essential for a structured, top-
down approach. PSL/PSA (11) is being tried out by
Centrum Voor Informatieverwerking (CVI) as a
support tool for SASO.

.4.   <u>Observations</u>.

SASO is probably one of the best documented and coordinated series of techniques for the logical and technical design of automated information systems in use today. It has been, and is still being, proved in practical working environments.

SASO is more than just a technique: it is also a philosophy which should be used as a continuous background concept during the application of the techniques.

This implies that thorough preparation, education and coaching should precede implementation. It is therefore a pleasant and necessary extra that excellent courses are available for the logical and technical design phases of SASO (of 10 and 5 days respectively).

Apart from these a programming course is available covering the Jackson interface to SASO.

A limited amount of coaching is being supplied by IBM-Netherlands.

References.

1)   IBM-course SASO-EA03-0, 1981 Systeemontwikkeling smethodiek delen I en II.

2) M. Lundeberg   A systematic approach to Information-systems development, part I and II University of Stockholm, May 1978.

3) E. Yourdon   Structured Design 1978.
   L.L.Constantine

4)   IBM-manuals GE20-0527.

5)   Metaplan-Novicursus,1981

6) C.J. Date   "An introduction to data base systems". Addison-Wesley Publ. Co. 1977.

7)   ISO-TC97/SC5/WG3. Concepts and Terminology for the Conceptual Schema and the Information Base, March 1981.

8) M.Jackson Systems Ltd.-JSD Tutorial, 1981

9) W. Kent   Developement of a data-description tool based on Entity-Relationship Concepts, August 6,1981

10) G.M. Nijssen   A conceptual Framework for Organisational Aspects of Future Data Bases.

11) D.Teichrew   Manuals PSL/PSA version 5.2, University of Michigan, 1981

3.6. NIAM

.1. Outline of the methodology.

.1.1. Philosophy.

NIAM stands for Nijssen's Information Analysis Methodology". Its aim is to systematically analyse and document all elements relevant in an area in which a computerized information system is to be operated so that it forms a complete and unambiguous basis for straightforward systems design. Elements analyzed are things like object types, the names assigned to them, the types of relation between them, restrictions, processes and integrity screening procedures. Basically the method describes a data dictionary/directory for the development, production and maintenance of administrative information systems.
An automated administrative information system is treated as a special tool for formalized delayed communication between human beings in an organization. Communication between people is most commonly effectuated by the natural language of which the sentence is the essential carrier. The basic thought is to register those sentences into the information system, which deal with essential things and happenings in the organisation.
"All allowed communication between an user and the information system is to be considered as a collection of selected sentences from the natural language" (ENALIM AXIOME).
The sentences are derived from the natural language and formalized in such a way as to uniquely define all concepts about things, concrete or abstract, and the relations between them.
In this way the intelligent "layman" is capable of modelling his environment to his own purpose and define his needs for information in a comprehensive, communicative and unambiguous way. One of the main purposes of the methodology is to invoke the user directly in systems design and indeed to make it possible for him to carry his responsibilities.

Any information system knows statical and dynamical aspects. The statical aspect is concerned with the definition of concepts used in the organisation and describes the status of the

138

object system at a certain point in time. This is
described in the so-called "information base".
The dynamical aspect describes how information
flows through the organization and what triggers
exist or are needed to get things going.

.1.1.1 The statical aspect.

This aspect is called ENALIM, Evolving Natural
Language in Information processing.
The definition and set-up of an information base
is the cornerstone of the NIAM-methodology.
Information is defined as a set of related
sentences which satisfy a certain set of rules or
grammar.
This set of rules should be fully understood,
agreed upon and accepted by the whole organization.

The following concepts are introduced:
a. The information base.The information base or
   sentence base is the container of allowed
   sentences.
The information base contains sentences about the
behaviour of the objectsystem, sentences about
the permissibility and semantics of sentences.

b. Sentences. The sentence is the basic construct
   in the methodology.
Non-elementary sentences are decomposed into
elementary sentences. An elementary sentence is a
sentence which cannot be decomposed without
losing vital information. The restriction to
elementary sentences implies that the information
base consists of only logical units of information. As a consequence the information base is
easier to maintain in case of structural changes
and easier to guard against inconsistencies.
A sentence is constructed in the following way:
- Every sentence refers to one or more objects,
  sentences relate objects.
- The semantic meaning of a sentence is related
  to linguistics by:
  1.The sentence name, which refers to the nature
    of the relation e.g. in "John works for
    Harry" works-for is the name of the sentence.
  2.The specific role the objects play in the
    relation. The role discriminates the object
    from other objects of the same type. In the
    example "John works for Harry" the person

with the name John plays the role of employee while the person with the name Harry clearly plays the role of an employer.

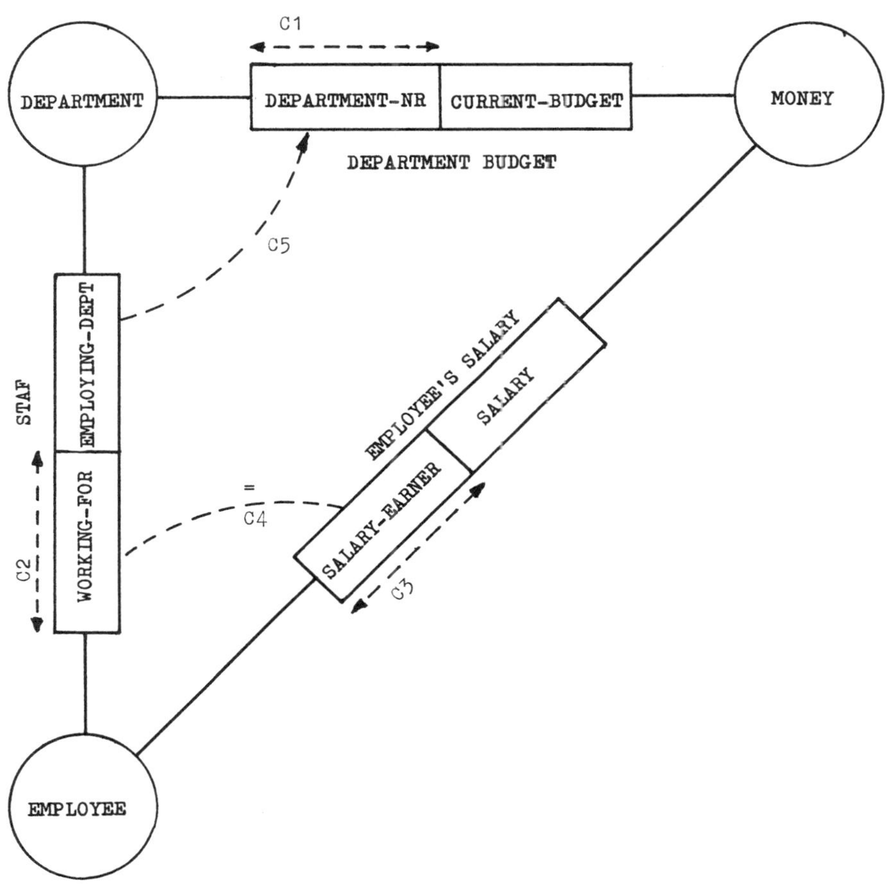

Figure 3.6.1 Sentences in NIAM.

c. The conceptual transaction. In NIAM information is defined as "a set of one or more related sentences which satisfy a certain set of rules or grammar". A conceptual transaction is the action of adding or deleting a set of related sentences derived from things that happened in a real or postulated world to or from the information base under the strict regulation of a set of rules which controls the integrity of the information base. Those rules are called constraints.

d. Information processes.

Some names assigned to sentences, object types etc. are obvious, others are clear by looking at the relations with other sentences and the constraints imposed on them.
Other sentences, called "derived sentences" are to be defined and calculated by a named algorithm that manipulates sentences already present in the information base. By those manipulating processes new terms are "learned" by the information system. The name of the algorithm represents a concept used in the organisation (e.g. profit).
Virtually all computations lead to results that should be defined as derived sentences in the information base. In theory all computations may be executed under the control of the information base handler in stead of by an application program..
Based upon this philosophy the remaining tasks of application programs consist of the care for input-output and editing.

e. Architecture.

NIAM distinguishes between the description of the information, the presentation of information and the storage of data. This is called the coexistence architecture which contains:

1. The conceptual schema. The conceptual schema is a contract between users of the information base. It is a prescriptive grammar which specifies what sentences are permitted in the information base.
The conceptual schema distinguishes between object types in the object system (NOLOTS, Non Lexical Object Types) and the way objects are addressed to (LOTS, Lexical Object Types). "Every sentence has a deep structure that exists of a collection of idea's about objects and a collection of bridges that relate the idea about objects with the names they are referred by." (SENE AXIOME)

2. The internal schema., which is a set of rules describing how information of the conceptual information base is physically represented in storage media.

3. The <u>external schema</u> is a description of how a
   user can see a subset of each conceptual
   schema instantiation.

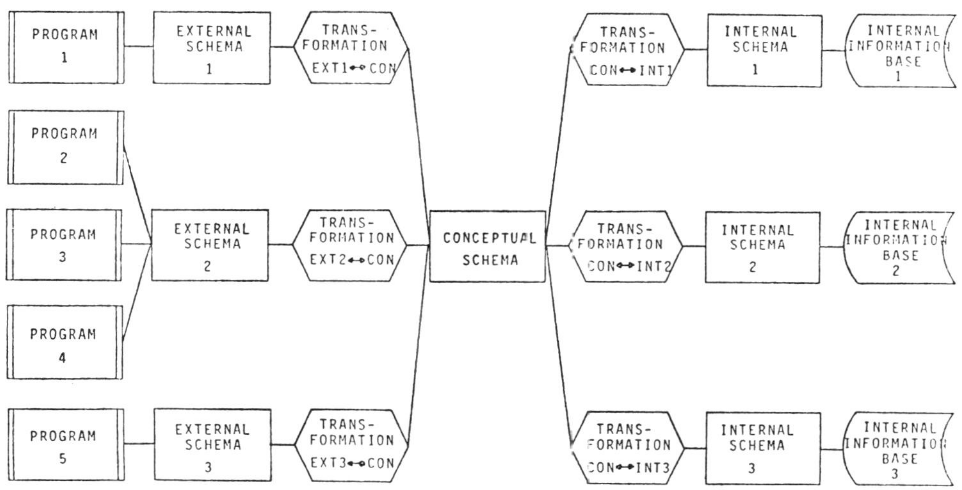

<u>Figure 3.6.2</u> Coexistence architecture.

The architecture allowes distributed storage,
distributed processing and a variability in user
views (see figure 3.6.2)
The three schemata and the data itself form the
information base.

The conceptual schema forms the data dictionary
of the organisation. Only one conceptual schema
exists. It is a complete set of rules for the
organisation as a whole.

f. The meta conceptual schema.

The behaviour of the information base (as a reflection of the behaviour of the organisation) is controlled by rules contained in the three schemata. This set of rules is itself documented in a meta information base, controlled by a so-called meta conceptual schema.
The conceptual, internal and external schemata are data to the meta conceptual schema. This meta level is constructed exactly conform the same coexistence architecture (see e.).
In this way the method is self contained and consistent. Modifications on the schemata are modifications, additions and deletions in the meta information base.

The collection of applications that maintain the meta information base is called "information dictionary" system and is comparable with what is generally understood with the terms "data-dictionary/directory system".
The meta information base may contain rules concerning control and administration of the base and its use like access-control, update-control, contentions, back-up-recovery etc. (see figure 3.6.3).

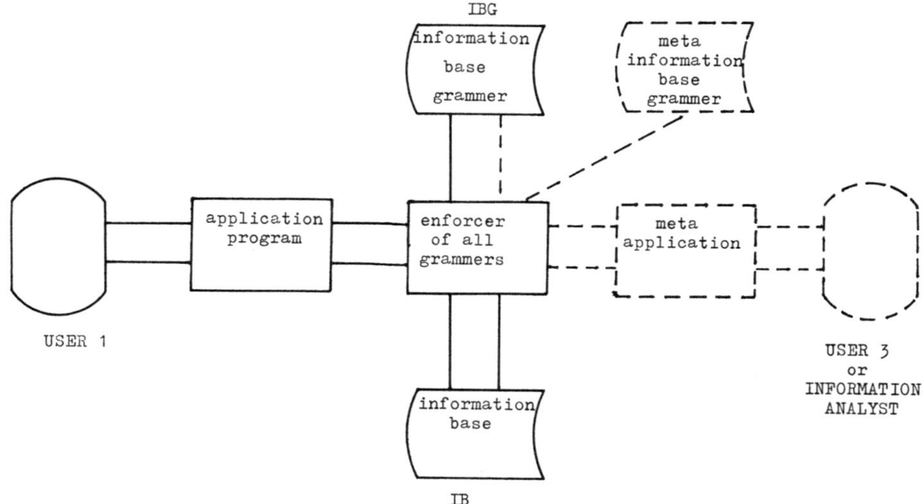

Figure 3.6.3 Information dictionary.

.1.1.2 The dynamical aspects.

The dynamics of an information system are the natural translation of the dynamics in the object system. By consequence the description of the information system dynamics is the description of the dynamical behaviour of the object system.
The dynamics of the object system is graphically recorded in an "information flow diagram" (IFD). The components of an IFD are:

- the information base. Only one logical information base is considered for an organisation.

- processes and functions. A process is something that transforms input into output following well defined rules. It is repeatable and has a begin and end (start-stop). If one abstracts from time a process is called a function.

- information flow. An information flow is a collection of sentences of one or more sentence types that are communicated between the components of the object system. In object system analysis this notation is used to represent the flow of material.

- Sources and sinks. Units outside the system under consideration that generate or absorb information flows and flows of materials.

IFD's are analysed following a top-down approach starting from one object- or information system. The methods used are decomposition and abstraction. The maximum level of detail is reached when processes and information flows are recognised as transactions.
In NIAM a transaction is a collection of processes related by order, repetition and selection at execution. A process is defined by the input and output flow.
A transaction is always started with a specific event and always completely executed. This is the basic framework for interconsistency control within the hierarchy of IFD's given by NIAM. The analytical scalpel is the transaction.

Implications of the concepts.

- Screening of the data is performed by the conceptual schema processor. It accepts or rejects transactions on the information base. Screening is no longer performed by the applications.

- A great number of computations and derivations are performed by the conceptual schema processor as a direct consequence of the derived sentence construction. The procedures that are needed for this can be programmed independently.

- Addition of elementary sentence types to the conceptual schema have no effect on the design of running applications, as well as modifications on the storage structure, hardware etc.

- Decomposition results in adding more elementary sentences. The result is the sum of the parts and theoretically independent of how the analysis is performed (department oriented, function oriented etc.)

1.2. Working procedure

The following main tasks are recognized (see fig. 3.6.4).

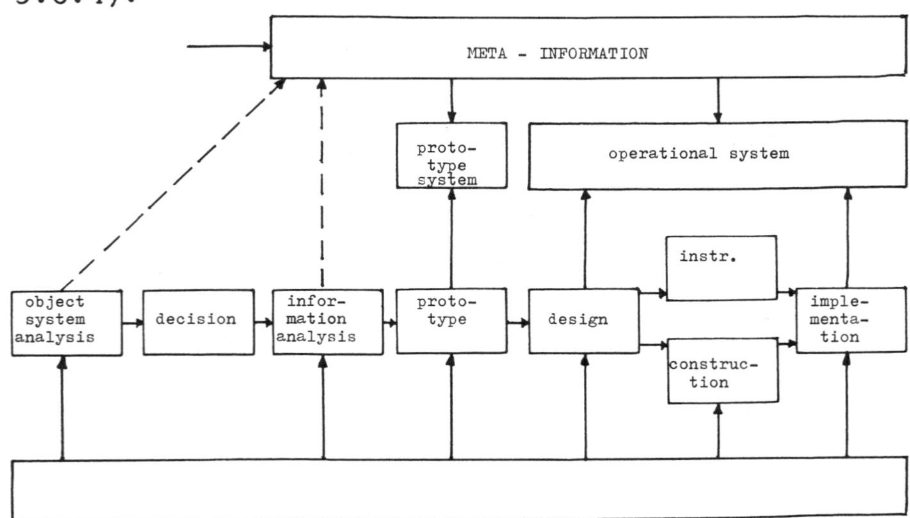

Figure 3.6.4 NIAM phases.

.1.2.1 Object system analysis

a. Definition of the scope of the analysis.
The method starts when the organization enters a new market, new techniques are introduced, new challenges are met or certain problems are felt in the organization. A restrictive framework is established to limit the scope of the analysis. Funds and organization are allocated.

b. Recognition of the company's primary processes.
Only those processes that directly contribute to the primary goals of the organization are considered. The organisation, geographical locations etc. and administrative processes are left out of the scope. In cases where information processing is the main task this distinction is often difficult. In such cases it is possible to automate the object system itself. This is called "process automation". In other cases the methodology speaks of "administrative automation".
The object system analysis starts with an IFD of the main production and information processes, flows of material and information and the interfaces with the environment (suppliers, clients etc.). The processes are decomposed into a hierarchy of less complex production units and activities. The maximum level of detail is reached when the activities are considered as one unit or must be executed without interruption. The main object types and their relations are recognized and analyzed.
The techniques used are decomposition and abstraction.

c. Determination of the information needs.
Once the primary processes are established the next step is to determine what (additional) information is needed to start, execute and control these processes at the lowest level in the structure.
In many cases the starting point will be the analysis of existing administrative processes.
All kinds of forms, lay-outs of files, computer output are collected and analysed.

146

.1.2.2 Project selection

d. Decision making.
Now a decision is made about what parts of the
IFD's are going to be automated and what problems
are going to be resolved by organisational
changes. The method is not concerned with the
practice of organisational changes.

.1.2.3 Information analysis.

e. Recognition of the information processes.
Information processes have to contribute to the
object system. The starting point is an IFD with
one primary process and the related incoming and
outgoing information flow. This IFD is decomposed
into a hierarchy of IFD's. Decomposition is
stopped when the information flow going in and
out of a process is recognized as a natural
cluster of data, such as an output report.
In many cases, of course, there is a great resem-
blance with existing forms and activities.

f. Construction of the conceptual grammar.
  -The input-output specifications from step e
  (reports) are transformed into a collection of
  elementary sentence types.
  -Indentifier constraints, subset constraints
  etc. are added.
 -abstract from naming conventions.
 -check the conceptual schema with the object
  system analysis. They must be consistent.
 -add structural constraints.
  Note: They are independent of the organisa-
         tional procedures.

g. Process description.

  Define per process how input is transformed
  into output. In this step some additional
  constraints are found. They are related to the
  procedures in the user organisation.

h. Define transaction descriptions.

  In this step "NIAM-processes" are aggregated
  to "transactions". Figures concerning the use
  of transactions in terms of frequencies, quantities, response times etc. are established

and recorded in an IFD per transaction.
Working procedures within the organization are
the glueing factor.

i. Prototype building.

With real life data collected from the object
system the information system is simulated and
the information base grammar is checked. This
can be done in the form of a desk check or, in
cases where the impact on the organisation is
unpredictable or heavy investments are needed,
by the creation of a working prototype.
The selection of those IFD's that were to be
automated is confirmed and scheduled and a
policy with respect to implementation is established.

.1.2.4 Design phase.

j. Construction of records.

In this step the conceptual model is transformed
into a technical model. Elementary sentences are
combined into ISAM-like records. This process is
called "grouping". Those records are easily
transformed into Codasyl, IMS or ISAM-like
structures.

k. Decomposition of processes.

Information processes resulting from the analysis
phase are decomposed into elementary processes.
Of every transaction it is determined in what
order what elementary processes are executed.

.1.2.5 Next steps.

The next steps are indicated but not substruc-
tured in the methodology.
- establishing form lay-out
- hardware/software selection
- administrative procedures, in this case the
  administration is the object system.
- development of user manuals
- construction phase
- instruction
- implementation.

.1.3 Documentation methodology.

In the conceptual schema the following graphical symbols are used:

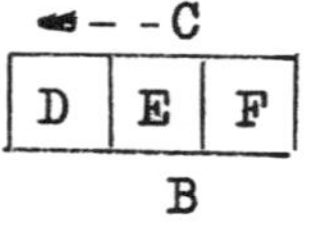

object-name type with name A

object-type with name A

Indication of a sentence type with name B in which three objects play the roles of D, E and F respectively

Identifier constraint with the name C. Defines what role or combination of rules uniquely defines a sentence occurrence.

Connector. Identifies what object plays what role in a sentence.

Information flow diagrams (IFD).

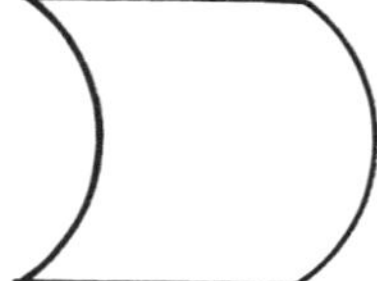

Process or function

Information flow. In the object system a flow of goods.

Source or sink.
They are generators or absorbers of information or supplies.

Information base. Only one information base is allowed for an organisation. If an IFD contains more then one such a symbol reference is made to the same information base.

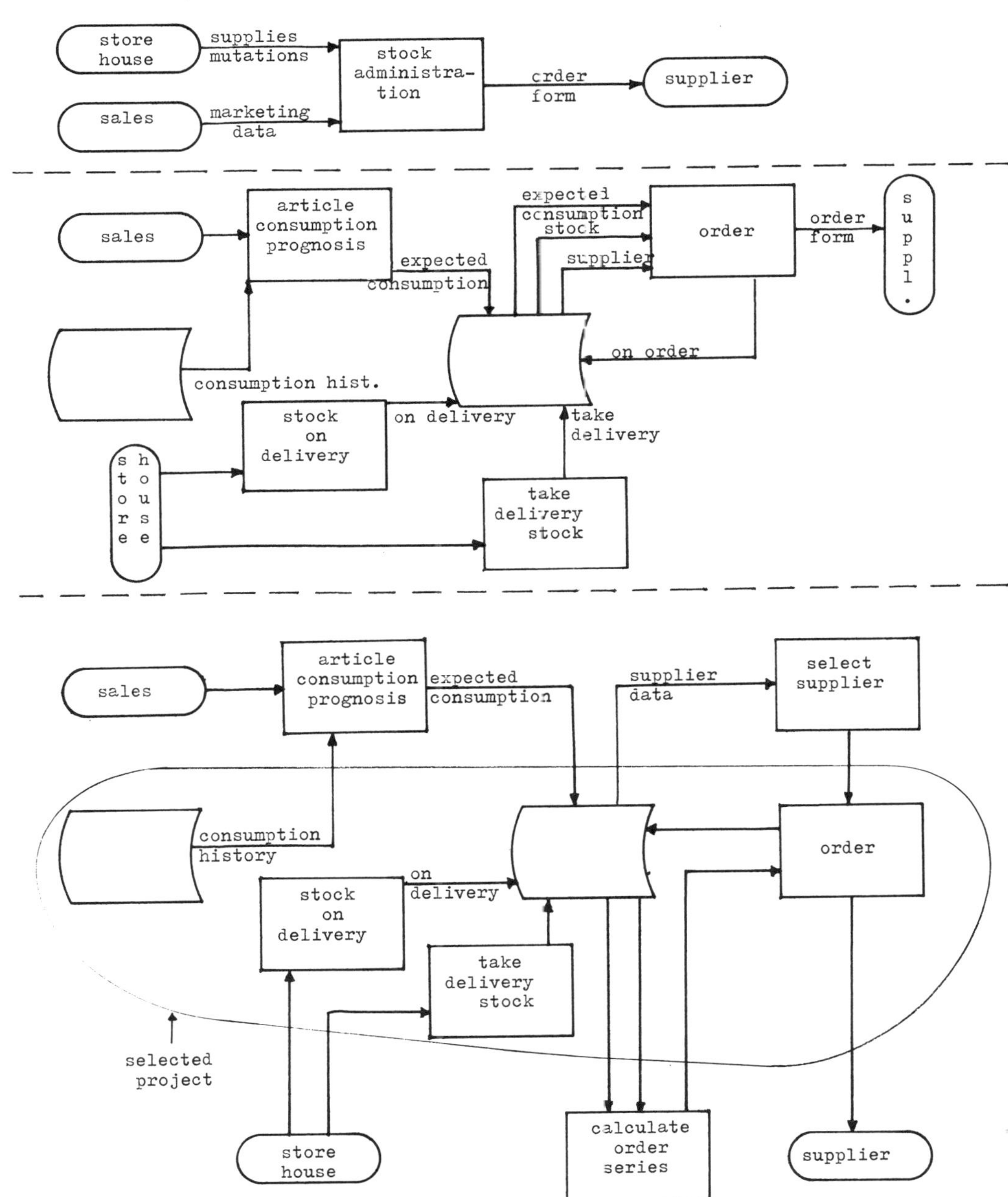

Figure 3.6.5   An example IFD.

150

<u>.1.4 Project management methodology.</u>

The effect of a good project management methodology greatly depends on both the flexibility and
formality of the design methodology
-   independently constructable subsystems
-   interdisciplinary collaboration
-   use of specialists on very narrow trajects
-   clear definition of the responsabilities in
    the various stages of the design.

NIAM does not include a project management methodology but in general it will be easily connected
to existing project management methodologies.
The main argument for this is the independence
between data definition, data manipulation, data
storage and maintenance.
In theory the design phases are well defined with
a good interrelation.

.2. <u>Evaluation-matrix NIAM.</u>

		philosophy	working procedure	documentation method			project-management method
				tech	org	cont	
Company analysis/ synthesis	1.1						
	1.2						
	1.3						
project-selection							
Logical design	3.1	▨	▨	▨		▨	
	3.2						
Logical → technical	4.1	▨	▨	▨		▨	
	4.2						
Technical design	5.1	▨	▨	▨		▨	
	5.2						
Physical design	6.1						
	6.2						
	6.3						
	6.4						
implementation							
exploitation							

.3 Applicability of the methodology

.3.1 Description of the matrix coverage.

.3.1.1 Corporate analysis and synthesis.

The NIAM methodology effectivily starts at the description of the object system. Continuity of the organisation, especially the analysis of necessary changes in the object system to meet changes in the external world are not discussed except in the case where the object system is an information process. Such a case is called "process automation".
In this phase the method is not computer-oriented. It cannot be because it is concerned with the companies information needs, not data processing. The needed level of detail is fairly well and operationally defined.

.3.1.2. Project selection

Project selection is explained in rather general terms. Documents created in the object system analysis phase are used to define and document coherent projects.

.3.1.3. Logical design.

Process and information analysis are described in detail. The method is only indirectly concerned with the design of administrative procedures in the user organisation. The main purpose is the realisation of an integrated information base with belonging tools and maintainable applications.
Conversion considerations and its effect on the design are not discussed.

.3.1.4 Conversion from logical to technical design.

One of the basic assumptions is that it is possible in a not too far away future to generate application programs and data storage structures from logical design specifications. Manually

executed conversion of data structures is indeed
rather simple. Conversion of processes lacks
criteria. The proto-type construction checks the
feasability of the results thus far with real
life data (and real life omissions).

.3.1.5 Technical design.

Transactions, computations, screening, elementary
processes and other components are structured on
the basis of frequencies of use, quantities,
geographical considerations etc.
The method ends where specific choices for hardware and system-software have to be made.

.3.1.6 Physical design.

The method is not specific about this and
following phases.

.3.2 Thoroughness of the methodology

When understood and properly followed the NIAM
methodology leads in an efficient way to detailed
and flexible maintainable results. The resulting
information system is minimal dependent upon the
structure of the user organisation. Up to the
technical design the method is rather complete
except for the strategy concerning the necessary
changes in the user organisations. This may lead
to problems in the user organisation when the
system is to be implemented.
The method is data driven. The interconsistency
and time invariance of the resulting information
system are in theory fairly good. The data
dictionary is the cornerstone of the method.

.3.3 Row transition.

The method is recursive. Its concepts are applicable in nearly every stage of realisation.
The coexistence architecture, focal point of the
methodology, formalizes the distinction between
the description of the company model, the interaction with the resulting information system and
considerations with respect to the realization

and maintenance phases.
Results from former steps are input and checks
for the next steps. From the description of the
company model unto the technical design, the
steps are closely linked with respect to information processes and the semantics of data.
The methodology lacks criteria in the area of
operations (back-up/recovery etc.) and ergono-
metry of the resulting information system. When
properly applied the methodology leads to formalized or formalizable procedures in the construction (files and programs) and maintenance phases,
resulting in a considerable reduction in costs.
Implementation is not covered.

.3.4 Column coordination.

The philosophy and working procedure are
consistent, although the philosophy covers a
broader terrain.
The documentation technique and content are
sufficient and satisfactory.
There are no standard forms.
The organization of the documentation and project
management aspects are not covered.
The methodology is not concerned with aspects
like cost/benefit analysis, financial decision
points and quality review points.

.4 Observations.

- A crucial point in the method is the transition from object system analysis to process
  and information analysis. The methodology is
  rather confusing on this point.

- The method makes no distinction between constraints that can be overruled or easily
  altered and constraints with a permanent
  character. The distinction between rules set
  by the physical laws governing the object
  system and rules (arbitrarely) set by the
  management is paramount. If not done with the
  utmost concern, this may lead to unnecessary
  detail in the logical design phase and less
  flexible maintainable applications in a latter
  stage.

- It is often more straightforward to combine process analysis, information analysis and input-output analysis in one step to minimize redundant explications from the user.

- The method is based on natural language. Non-information technicians tend to grasp the method more easily and less reluctant than information specialists. The user tends to be more active and more aware of his responsibility.

- The NIAM method is affiliated with the ANSI-SPARC and ISO-TC97/SC5-WG3 proposals.

- NIAM claims that its approach reduces programming efforts and maintenance cost by a factor 2-4.

- As long as the, in the idea's of NIAM, needed transformation processors are not commercially available, they will have to be realized in the applications programs.
  The problem then will be to communicate the concepts to the programming staff. Unnoticed deviations from the concepts will lead easily to reduced maintainability and flexibility.

- The method supposes full agreement on the conceptual grammar with all the management staff. It is very questionable whether this is necessary.

156

<u>References</u>

1) G.M.Nijssen   Workshop Data Base Technologie, Control Data, Brussels, 1977.

2) G.M.Nijssen   On the gross architecture for the next generation data base management systems, Control Data, Europe, 1977.

3) G.M.Nijssen   Integratie Informatiesystemen en informatiebasis, Informatie no. 4, 1977. (in Dutch)

4) E.A.Nijmeijer   Higher programming efficiency through better data base concepts. Infotech Conference, Copenhagen, October 1977

5)   Data Base The Next Five Years, Infotech, Londen, December 1977.

6) G.M.Nijssen   Workshop Information Analysis, Data Base Design and Inplementation, Control Data, Brussels, May 1978.

7) G.M.Nijssen   A Conceptual Framework for Organizational Aspects of Future Data Bases, Control Data, Brussels, September 1978

8) G.M.Nijssen   A framework for advanced mass storage applications, Control Data and University of Brussels, February 1980.

9) G.M.A. Verheijen J.van Bekkum   Nijssens Informatie-Analyse-Methode (NIAM) Informatie 1/1982 (in Dutch)

3.7. BUBBLE-CHARTING.

.1. Outline of the methodology.

.1.1. Philosophy

The "bubble-charting" (BC) methodology is based on the idea of functional dependence between data elements (1, 6, 8, 10, 11). Data-element can be classified as:

- identifiers (primary keys)
- attributes.

This system of classifying elements as either keys or attributes is also one of the basic principles of the normalisation procedures first advocated by T.Codd.
The only difference between the "bubble-charting" procedures and the normalisation procedures is the point at which analysis starts.
In normalisation , this starting point is the unnormalised "information pool", whereas "bubble-charting" starts from the information requirements as seen by the end-user.
These information requirements (IR's) are expressed in print layouts, VDU screens messages etc., and they tend to be very end user oriented.
The BC-methodology can therefor be characterised as output-oriented (1, 6)
To represent the data elements concerned, BC, which is also known as canonical data-structuring (6), uses circular bubbles. Arrows are used to show the dependencies which exists between data-elements (fig. 1)

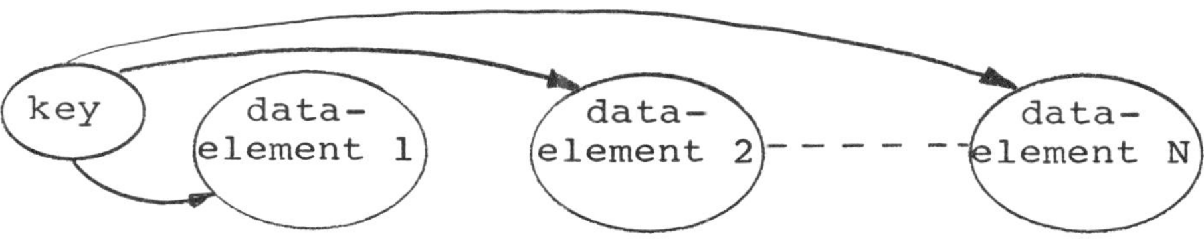

fig. 1

Single arrows indicate that key A uniquely identifies elements B and C (fig. 2)

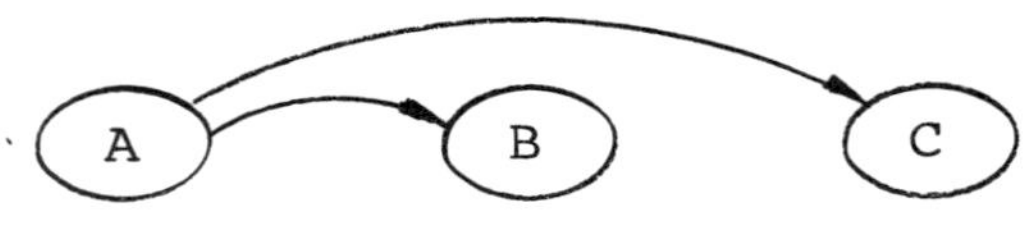

fig. 2

The above also tells us that B and C are func-
tionally dependent on A.

Definition: A primary key (A in fig. 2) is a data
element having one or more outgoing
single arrows.
An attribute is a data element having
no outgoing single arrows (6).

Dependencies may also exist between keys themselves (fig. 3).

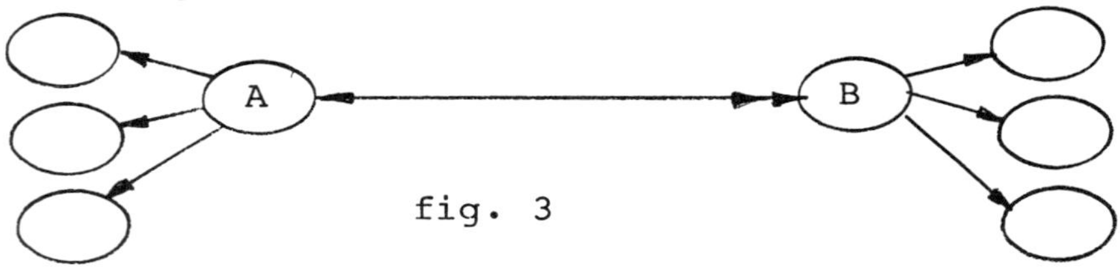

fig. 3

A double arrow at B means that the relationship
type between A and B is one to many (1 to N).

<u>Main keys and Secondary keys.</u>

Primary keys may identify attributes or other
primary keys as shown by a single outgoing arrow.
Primary keys without outgoing single arrows
toward other primary keys are <u>main keys.</u>
An information element that does not uniquely
identify another element will be called
<u>secondary key.</u> Secondary keys are indicated by an
outgoing double arrow.
Dependencies which are superfluous can be removed
on condition that they do not provide additional
informational (fig. 4).

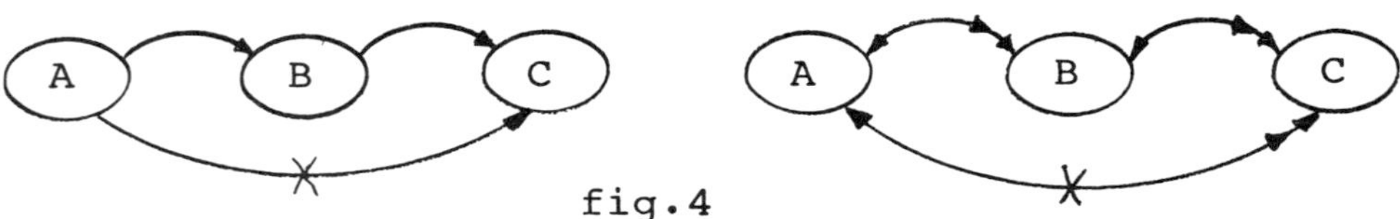

fig.4

.1.2. Working procedure

.1.2.1. Information recording and requirements

Before any BC exercise can be started, all the user's Information Requirements (IR's) must first be collected.
An IR specification must contain a description of:

- the objective: what is this IR used for and how will this IR accomplish any user needs

- the data structure: (repeating groups, sorts),

- all relevant data elements.

.1.2.2. Working procedure (6)

To find the intrinsic data structure of an IR, the following procedural steps should be used:

1. Establish the first normal form for any chosen information structure (IR), according to the normalisation rules of Codd. When this is done the IR should contain no repeating groups, or repeating groups within repeating groups.

2. Draw the IR as a bubble-chart. Compound keys are shown as one bubble and the constituent keys themselves are shown as separate bubbles. An example is shown in fig. 5.
   Process-elements (derived elements) are reduced to their elementary basic attributes.

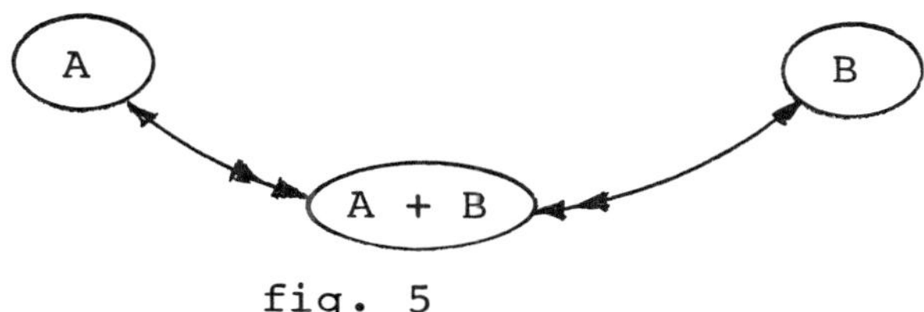

fig. 5

The preceding steps mean that the BC need only show 1:1 and 1:n dependencies.

3. Establish the first normal form for the next
   IR, repeat step 2 and add the result to the
   existing bubble-chart. Care should be taken to
   identify any homonyms or synonyms.

4. Indicate which bubbles represent primary keys.

5. Where dependencies between primary keys occur,
   both directions should be indicated. In following these procedures, all m to n dependencies
   will be replaced by separate 1:n dependencies
   and the relevant compound keys (fig. 6).

fig. 6

6. Remove superfluous dependencies if those do
   not have additional informational meaning.

7. Repeat steps 3 up 6 for all Information Requirement structures.

8. Check the final bubble-chart (the total integration of all individual bubble-charts) for
   any appearance of intersection attributes, and
   remove these by:

   - replacement of the dependency via existing
     keys
   - duplication of the data
   - addition of a new key.

9. Check the final B-C for appearances of single
   attributes to make sure that these are not the
   result of interpretation failures.

10. Re assemble (group) the data, and draw the
    final data structure.

11. Finally check to see which dependencies
    between the previous established groups can be
    removed without loosing information sense.

12. Indicate all secondary keys in the relevant
    dependencies.
    (A secondary key is an attribute with one or
    more outgoing double arrows).

.1.3.   Documentation method

In bubble-charting the following symbols are used.

   elements (keys and attributes)
Note: keys should be hatched.   

   functional dependencies

———▸▸   1 to N

◂◂——▸▸   N to M (which will later be split into two relationships)

◂———▸▸   functional dependence between two keys

The transformation into a Bachman diagram is done in the following way:

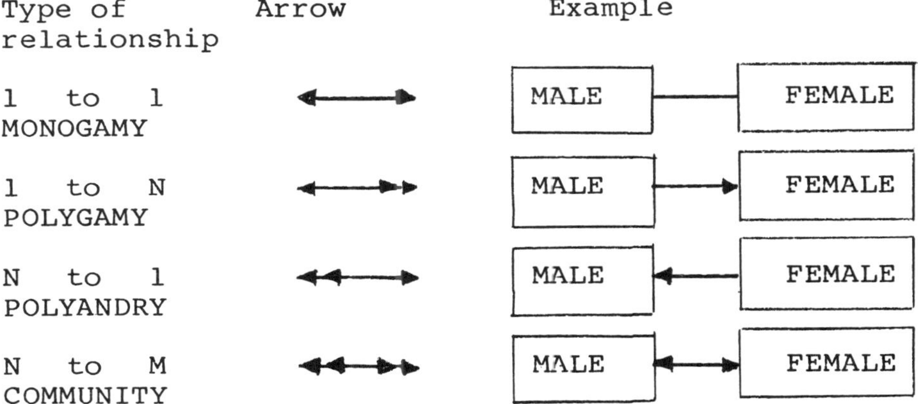

Type of relationship	Arrow	Example	
1 to 1 MONOGAMY	◂———▸	MALE	FEMALE
1 to N POLYGAMY	◂——▸▸	MALE	FEMALE
N to 1 POLYANDRY	◂◂——▸	MALE	FEMALE
N to M COMMUNITY	◂◂——▸▸	MALE	FEMALE

.1.4. Projectmanagement method

The logical data structuring activities of bubble-charting is done in parallel with the functional design activities as outlined in SDM phases 2.3, 2.4 and 2.6. However, because this BC methodology is output oriented, these activities must be done <u>after</u> the functional analysis phase.

BC has been assigned to SDM's phase 2.9: "structure of the logical data-collection". The grouping of entities and the transformation into Bachman diagrams is done in SDM's logical-technical phase 3.3.

During the fysical DB design stage, it may be necessary to examine individual IR's to see precisely how the data is used. This becomes necessary when physical structures force the designer to deviate from the logical data structure design.

Note: SDM stands for "System Development Methodology". It is marketed by Pandata systems home Holland and it includes bubble-charting in its range of techniques.

.2.   <u>Evaluation-matrix B.C.</u>

		philosophy	working procedure	documentation method			project-management method
				tech	org	cont	
Company analysis/ synthesis	1.1						
	1.2						
	1.3						
project-selection							
Logical design	3.1						
	3.2	////	////	////	////	////	
Logical → technical	4.1						
	4.2	////	////	////	////	////	
Technical design	5.1						
	5.2						
Physical design	6.1						
	6.2						
	6.3						
	6.4						
implementation							
exploitation							

.3. Use of the methodology.

.3.1. Description of the matrix coverage.

The evaluation matrix shows that the columns of
"philosophy", "working procedure" and "documentation method" are covered.
In addition, practical experience shows that the
philosophy does support the working procedures,
and that these procedures are capable of genera-
ting the required documentation.
However since the objective of BC is to design a
logical DB-structure, it can also be employed in
the more technical project phases shown in the
lower rows of the evaluation matrix.

.3.2. Thoroughness of the methodology

Bubble-charting is based on the concept of functional dependence between data items.
("Functional" here has been used in the sense of
$y=f(x)$, where x is the identifying element)

This point is critical when it comes to discuss-
ing the thoroughness of the methodology. Even
though the theoretical definitions are unambiguous, it is still extremely difficult to identify functional dependencies in unstructured
information groups. BC gives the user a tool
which simplifies the task of identifying these
functional dependencies.
Practical experience shows that the application
of BC results in the production of very complete
problem solutions characterised by:

- a range of acceptable alternatives for the
  solution of the original problem(s),
- a data model which remains relatively stable
  even though the functional requirements may
  vary at a later date.

It would also appear that most current data analysis methodologies are essentially based on the
bubble-charting techniques.
Although the BC methodology is an excellent tool
for the development of stable solutions, as with
any methodology, the success of its use is limited by the ability of the analyst to understand
the data elements in the real world of the end

user (and, conversely, by the end user's knowledge of his own world).

.3.3. Row transition.

Bubble charting supports the development of a logical data model and this data model can then be converted directly into Bachman diagrams. The development of this logical model and the conversion to Bachman diagrams are independent procedural tasks.

.3.4. Column coordination.

A practical methodology can be characterised as having a "soft" or unnoticable transition between the columns "philosophy", "research method" and "documentation method". Experience with bubble-charting has shown that most relevant practical problems can be solved using guidelines set down in the BC philosophy. The working procedures automatically generate the required documentation.

.4. Interface to other analysis/design methods.

As stated previously, almost all data analysis methods are based on the principles of "precedence" or "functional" dependency.
Since the data analysis methods of Data and Codd are also based on the concept of functional dependency, they are equivalent to bubble charting described here. The proces analysis methods such as MOS, ISAC en Warnier are precedence oriented and do not lead directly to the production of a data model. However, the results obtained tend to supplement rather then to contradict the BC models.

<u>References.</u>

1) Date, C.J.   An introduction to database
                      systems, Addison-Weslet Publ.
                      Co., Reading Mass. 1975.

2) Bramhill, P.S.   Database design using Third
   Taylor, G.   Normal Form and Bachman dia-
                     grams, Database Journal vol.6
                     nr.12 (1975)

3) Bachman, Ch.W.   Data structure diagrams,
                     Database ACM-SIGBDP quarterly
                     vol.2 no.2 (1969)

4) Codd, E.F.   A relational model of Data
                     for large shared Databanks.
                     CACM 13, nr.6 (June 1970)

5) Codd, E.F.   Normalised Database Structure
                     A Brief Tutorial, Proc. 1971
                     ACM SIGFIDET.

6) James Martin   A procedure for canonical DB-
                     design, December 1976, Spea-
                     ker's paper.

7) James Martin   Computer Data Base Organisa-
                     tion, Prentice-Hall, New Jer-
                     sey, 1975.

8)   GH 20-1620 IBM manual.
                     Data Base Design Aid, Desig-
                     ners Guide.

3.8 Warnier-Orr

.1. Outline of the methodology.

.1.1.Philosophy

This methodology is based on the analysis of the
desired output such as tables, print lay-outs,
screen formats, etc. The output specifications
are analysed on the one hand with respect to
their content (what independent data elements are
necessary to produce the required output table)
and with respect to the functions which have to
be performed on the other. The functions have to
be analysed further and have to be specified.
The analysis of the functions is performed in
such a way that the final result can be transformed directly into input for the structured
programming process. The analysis uses the same
logical structures that are used in structured
programming. In addition to the functions
necessary to produce the required output,
functions which perform transactions on the
(logical) database also have to be analysed. The
relations between these and the (output)
functions have to be defined and described.

1.2. Working procedure

The design of systems including databases is
performed via the following steps:
- describe the logical, hierarchical structure
  of the desired output reports.
- describe the logical database required to
  generate the output reports. "Derived items"
  are to be avoided in this logical database.
- analyse the functions required to generate
  the output reports. Between the resulting
  function model and the logical database there
  should be an optimal correspondance.
- check whether or not the data in the logical
  database is already available somewhere else.
  If so, integrate the logical database with
  the relevant structures.
  > N.B. How this integration should be per-
  > formed is not described. Because of the
  > strict hierarchical structure of the logi-
  > cal database, conflicts may arise during
  > this integration process. The methodology
  > offers no solution for these problems. (See

> however the solution given by the Bubble Charting method)
> . determine the way the data elements in the logical database will be modified and describe the underlying "logical updating functions".
> . integrate these logical updating functions with the function model resulting from the functional output analysis.

The result of this integration corresponds directly to the information required for the structured programming and hierarchical database design processes. However, the translation from the logical database into a physical realisation will add some additional function steps to the function modelling process.

.1.3. Documentation method

Warnier diagrams are used as a tool to document the data structure and the function model, and as a means to communicate the results to the user. The distinction between these diagrams and other tools used to describe hierarchical structures, is that Warnier diagrams show certain logical operators in the diagrams themselves. These logical operators are the sequential, repetition and choice operator. To give an example, the same data structure will be shown twice, once using the Bachman notation technique and once representing it by using Warnier diagrams:

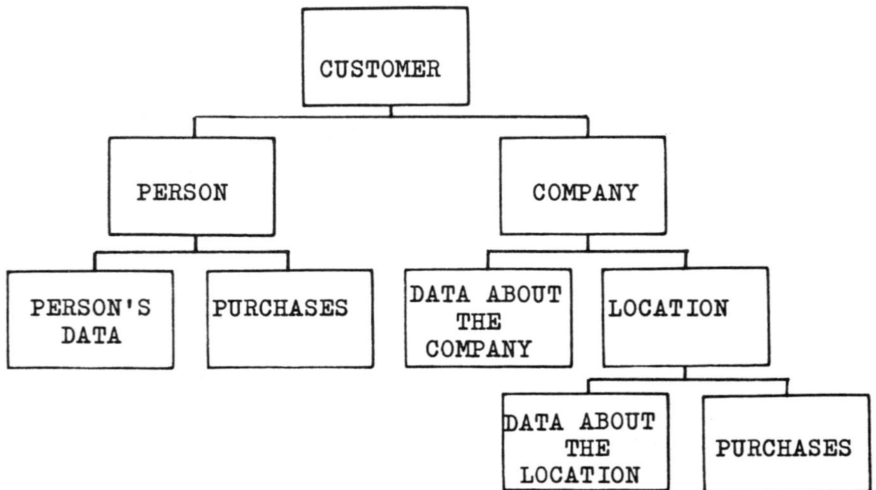

Figure 3.8.1 Bachman data structure

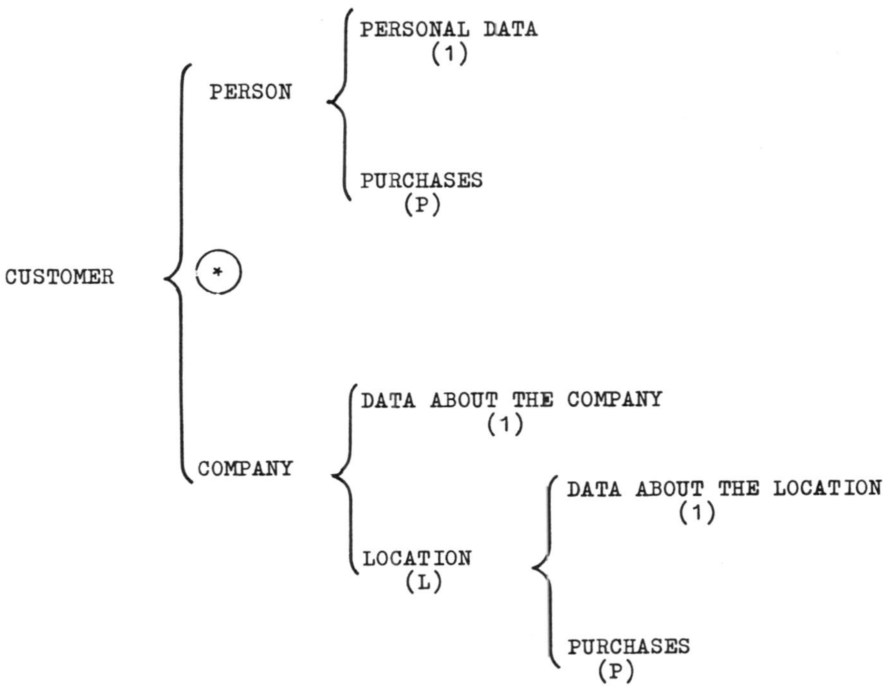

Figure 3.8.2 Warnier diagram

The symbol * represents the choice operator, (....) represents the repetition operator (so (P) means in this diagram P purchases, (L) means L locations etc.), { represents a subdivision and, in the case of the functional system description, it also describes the relative position of the function with respect to other sequences.

.1.4. The project management method.

The Warnier Orr methodology does not provide any facilities for project management. Instead, the project management method already used by the user should be applied. Implicitly, the Warnier Orr methodology does allow for achieving results in an iterative way. This may be a disadvantage for the management of the project.

.2. <u>Evaluation-matrix Warnier-Orr.</u>

		philosophy	working procedure	documentation method			project-management method
				tech	org	cont	
Company analysis/ synthesis	1.1						
	1.2						
	1.3						
project-selection							
Logical design	3.1						
	3.2						
Logical → technical	4.1						
	4.2						
Technical design	5.1						
	5.2						
Physical design	6.1						
	6.2						
	6.3						
	6.4						
implementation							
exploitation							

.3. Applicability of the methodology.

.3.1. Description of the matrixcoverage.

This methodology is primarily oriented towards the logical design of an information system. The use of logical operators provides a direct link to the process of physical systems realisation. However, only a hierarchical data model is supported. Moreover, the starting point for functional analysis is arbitrary. As a result, this methodology does not in any way support a strategy to structure the total information supply.

.3.2. Thoroughness of the methodology

It is up to the designer to determine the appropriate level of detail of the analysis. The only condition which has to be obeyed, is, that derived items must be eliminated. These items have to be analysed until the "basic" items are determined. The functions which are used to calculate these derived items have to be integrated into the function model. The scope of the analysis has to be determined by the user; no rules are given as how to do this.

.3.3. Row transition.

Because of the documentation method used, a direct link has been established between the output, logical design, the translation into the physical design and the actual building of the system.

.3.4. Column coordination.

The description of the functions and the data items is done by using the Warnier diagrams. This approach guarantees an optimal connection between the working procedure and the documentation of the results. It is claimed that the documentation format used also ensures a good communication with the actual user. Missing user requirements should be easily detected during the analysis phase and can be integrated into the system design in an iterative way.

.4. Observations.

Problems may arise due to the strict hierarchical modelling technique which is applied both to the data model and to the function model. Problems are bound to occur, especially in the case where the same data items occur in several different data structures.

The resulting network-like structures cannot be fully described by using the recommended documentation technique.

References.

1. Jean-Dominique Warnier   "L'organisation des donnees d'un systeme", Les Editions d'Organisation. 1974, Parijs.

2. Kenneth T. Orr   "Structured systems development", Yourdon Press, 1977 New York.

3. Ralph I. Prudkin   "Structured programming at work", Datamation, October 1979.

3.9. The Jackson Systems Development Methodology.

.1. Outline of the Methodology.

The Jackson Structured Programming method has been around now for quite some time. Its goal was to provide a methodical approach towards program design. The method is based on the following principles:
- the result of the design activity should be independent of inspiration of the designer i.e. it should be an objective and repeatable process.
- the design process should be manageable. This has to be achieved by phasing the design process.

Many organisations have gained experience in applying this method.

Only recently,the Jackson Structured Progamming methodology has been replaced (to a certain extent) by the Jackson System Development Methodology.

This latter methodology encompasses the first one.

.1.1.   Philosophy.

The basic assumption in the method is that it is possible to model the part of the world that is of interest to us in terms of entities and actions excluding functions. Entities are basic elements that the user can recognize e.g. customers, orders etc. Actions are performed on entities, and transform the entity from one state into another. These states are the different phases in the life-cycle of the entity (e.g. enrolling a staff member, promotion, retirement etc.). The execution of a function however, involves usually several entities and may or may not affect the states of these entities.

It is assumed that this model consisting of entities, actions and (as a glue) datastreams, is less vulnerable to evolution of the problem area than a model which incorporates actual functions to be performed. Functions are time-dependent where as the model is, to a certain degree, time-independent.

Functions are inserted on this model and certain measures are taken to guarantee a proper working

of the resulting model.
Strict separation between the design and implementation phase is attempted. Only in the last phase are characteristics of the hardware and software environment seen to be of relevance and to influence the results.
Because of the late stage in which computer-technical aspects are involved, the user has a large amount of influence on the design process. To facilitate this, the model is described in a formal and pictorial way.

.1.2. Working procedure.

Prior to the first stage in the method, a rough description should be available to delimit the problem area. However, no method to aid in the determination of the scope of the problem area is offered.
The methodology distinguishes the following steps:
- the entity/action step
- the entity structure step
- the initial model step
- the function step
- the system timing step
- the implementation step.
In principle, these steps should be performed in sequential order.

The entity/action step has multiple results. In this step, a determination is done and a description is acquired of all the relevant entities and actions in the problem area. The choice of entities is a relatively arbitrary one. Any "noun" may be selected. However, there are two conditions. First, the candidate entity should be either an object or a subject in any of the actions which are recognized. Secondly, the candidate entity should have a significant time dimension i.e. it should evolve in time in discrete steps. The specification of the relevant entities and actions is the first result.

In selecting the proper entities and actions, a further delimitation of the problem area is implicitly obtained. The fixation of the problem area and its boundary is the second result.
The second step in the design process is the

<u>entity structure step</u>. In this step a complete description is given of the life-cycle of all the selected entities and the allowable transitions from one stage in the life history of an entity into another one are determined.
The resulting entity structures are represented by using the same diagram technique as applied to data structures in the Jackson Structured Programming method. However, to be an acceptable structure, the entity structure should obey some basic rules:
- the structure has to mirror the behaviour of the real world entity it represents in allowing transitions from one stage into another one.
- the structure diagram should contain the minimum detail necessary to describe the real world entity.

In this way, for each entity (type) a structure is produced containing all conditions and processes which have to be executed to transcribe the relevant entity from one stage of the life cycle into another one. The actual information for each entity (occurrence) is stored in the associated state vector.

So far the entities have been regarded as mutually independent. Of course, in real world environment, there is an interdependency between the entities and an interaction between the entities and the real world itself. Glueing the entities together and embedding the result in the (real world) environment is the main goal of the third design step, the so-called <u>Initial Model</u> step. Each entity structure has to be identified in this step as a process with datastream or state vector connection either to a real-world entity which can provide its input, or to another process in the model. Datastreams are applied when an action on entity A results in actions on several other entities. Not all processes however are connected by datastreams. In some cases, the interdependency between the processes is based on inspection: the action of process B may be dependent on the state of process A or the actual information content of the entity A. So, in these cases before execution of B, A has to be inspected.

In this modelling step, the sources of the data-

streams to the processes need to be catagorised. The source may be internal (i.e. input from another process) or external (i.e. input from the real world). A special case of this latter category is the phenomenon of "time".
Coordination within the model is based on time. Time information is represented by Time Grain Markers.

So far, the resulting model does not produce any output to the real world and no (other) functions are available. The distinction between a function and an action is that a function is applied to the model created by the previous step, whereas an action is applied on a single entity. In this (fourth) step, functions are added to the model. Addition of functions to the model has to be done in decreasing order of complexity. This is done to decrease the number of changes to the model. In decreasing order of complexity, the following classes of functions are identified:
  -interacting functions. Addition of these requires the addition to the model itself of new function processes which generate data streams to existing processes.
  -imposed functions. New function processes which are connected by state vector inspection of existing processes are added to the model.
  -embedded functions. Addition of these functions only requires the embedding of output operations into existing model-processes.

Having added these functions to the model, we obtain a refined and updated model as well as a description of the output data streams.
Next step in the modelling is the <u>System Timing Step.</u>
In this step adequate measures are taken to ensure a correct scheduling of the system processes. For this purpose, synchronisation processes are defined. In these processes, synchronisation between the so far independently treated external time sources take place. Furthermore, the reaction of the relevant processes upon time information has to be specified. For example, sometimes it may be necessary to have an immediate reaction upon a "time pulse", such as moving to another process as soon as the time pulse arrives. In other cases, the moving to another

process may require the processing of all input stream data records which carry a time stamp prior to the time pulse.

The last step to be performed is the <u>Implementation step</u>. Ideally, all processes should be implemented on separate processors. However, this is not a practical solution. Resource sharing is the only realistic approach. Furthermore, the design process assumes that processes will run for as long as the associated entity exists in the real world. This assumption cannot usually be implemented in a practical situation. So transformations have to be applied to transform the ideal model into a realistic environment.
In these translations one also has to take into account further demands such as response times, limited resources, hardware-software and organisational constraints etc.
The transformations include program inversion with regard to one or multiple data streams, separation of state vectors, program dismembering etc. To account for scheduling, a separate program has to be developed.
As a result of the implementation step, one obtains
  - programs representing the processes to be performed
  - datafiles or databases in which the storage of the state vectors takes place.
  - a scheduling mechanism, possibly represented by a stream of Job Control Statements.

.1.3.   Documentation Method.

In the Jackson System Development Methodology the following terms are used:
  - System Specification Diagram (=SSD) showing the processes of the system and the connections among them.
  - System Timing Diagram (=STD), an SSD including Time Grain Markers, streams and the processes which write them.
  - System Implementation Diagram (=SID). This diagram shows how the system is implemented in terms of programs, procedures and data files adapted to the implementation environment.
  - Data Structure Diagram (=DSD). This is a tree structure diagram showing the structure of a

data stream. It is a familiar representation
of data structures in terms of sequence,
iteration and selection.
- Program Structure Diagram (=PSD) showing the
structure of a process. The same technique as
applied for DSD is used in PSD.
- Program Structure Text (=PST) is a textual
form of the PSD, written in Jackson Structured
Programming structure text, and including
conditions on iteration and selection components.

In a SSD the following set of symbols is used:

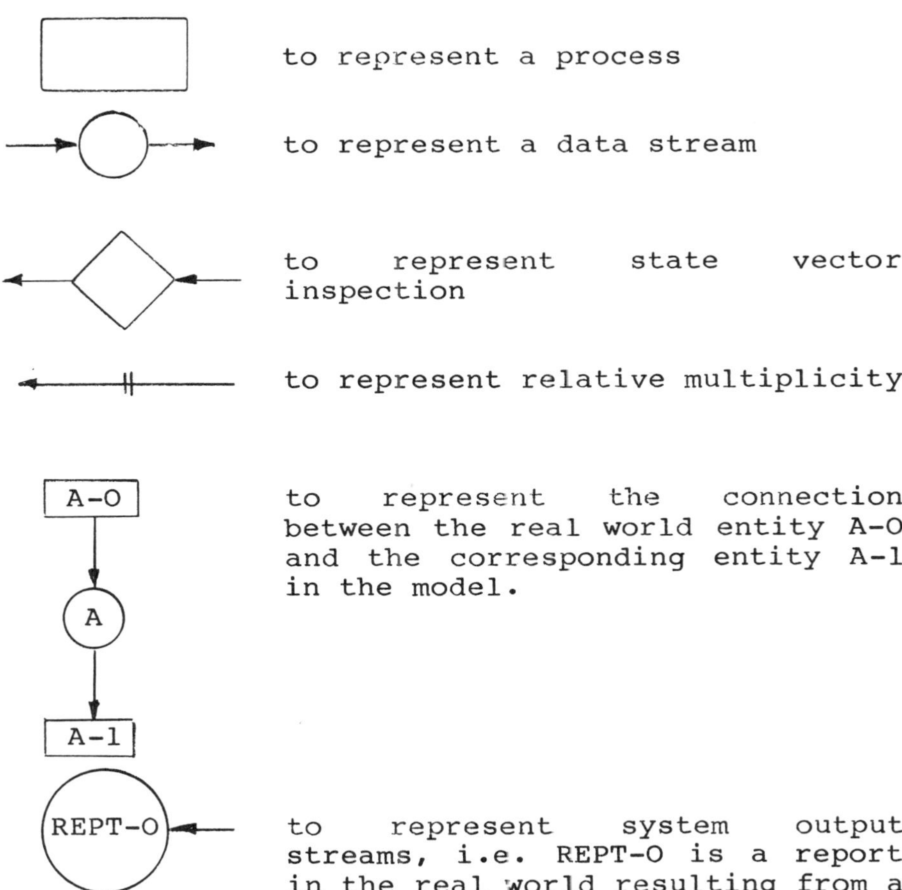

to represent a process

to represent a data stream

to represent state vector inspection

to represent relative multiplicity

to represent the connection between the real world entity A-0 and the corresponding entity A-1 in the model.

to represent system output streams, i.e. REPT-O is a report in the real world resulting from a process in the model.

Furthermore, the concept of Time Grain Markers is
used in the SSD.

In a Data Structure Diagram the familiar notation
for data structures is used. It includes four
component types: sequence, selection, iteration
and elementary.

Sequence:

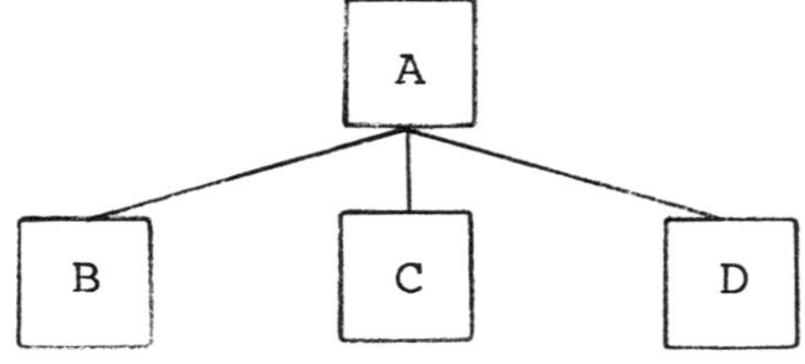

This diagram represents a component A consisting
of parts B, C and D. For each occurrence of A,
the parts B, C and D occur once each and in that
order.

Selection:

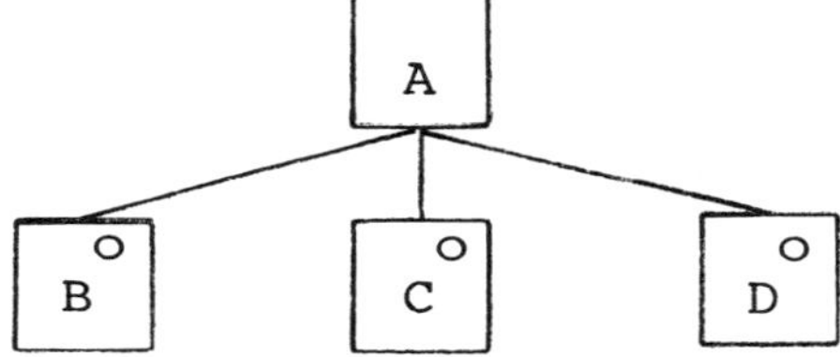

This diagram represents a component A consisting
of either part B, part C or part D. B, C and D
are exclusive of each other.

Iteration

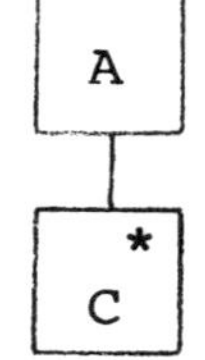

This diagram shows that for each occurence of A
the part C may occur an arbitrary number of
times.

Elementary

An elementary component has, by definition, no
parts. A special elementary component is the null
component or void component. This empty component
is represented by

Any DSD consists of a consistent combination of the four components as described above.

A PST (Program Structure Text) describes the same structure as a DSD, but uses a textual form of the program.
Corresponding to the four basic components used in DSD are the following texts:

Sequence

```
A    seq
     B
     C
     D
A    end
```

Selection

```
A    sel (condition-B)
     B
A    alt (condition-C)
     C
A    alt (condition-D)
     D
A    end
```

Iteration

```
A    itr while (condition-C)
     C
A    end
```

Elementary

    no representation because it is not an executable statement.

Conditions under which selections are made or iterations stay valid are explicitly mentioned in the PST but not in the DSD. Their sequence in the text is also the sequence in which they are executed in reality.

It is not always possible, with the information available at the moment when a decision should be taken, to select between parts or to decide whether or not to proceed with the iteration. In these cases it is supposed that the condition is

fulfilled and on this assumption the process
proceeds until it becomes obvious that the assumption was wrong and the condition was not
fulfilled. Then, conditionally or unconditionally
the process has to go back to the original
decision point. All actions performed so far have
to be eliminated.
This "retreat" process is called "backtracking".
It is represented in PST by using the noun
"quit".
The situations in which it may occur (namely in
two-part selections and iterations) are in PST
described as:

```
selection:  A posit
            B1
            A quit   (condition-not-bx)
            B2
            A quit   (condition-not-by)
            B3
            A admit
            C
            A end
```

Note: "sel" and "alt" have been replaced by
"posit" and "admit".

```
Iteration: A itr
            B1
            A quit   (condition-not-bx)
            B2
            A quit   (condition-not-by)
            B3
            A end
```

A System Timing Diagram is essentially a SSD
extended with information about all TGM (Time
Grain Marker) streams and the processes which
write them. A process which writes a TGM stream
is represented by a box (as an ordinary process)
but with a double bar on the lower edge.

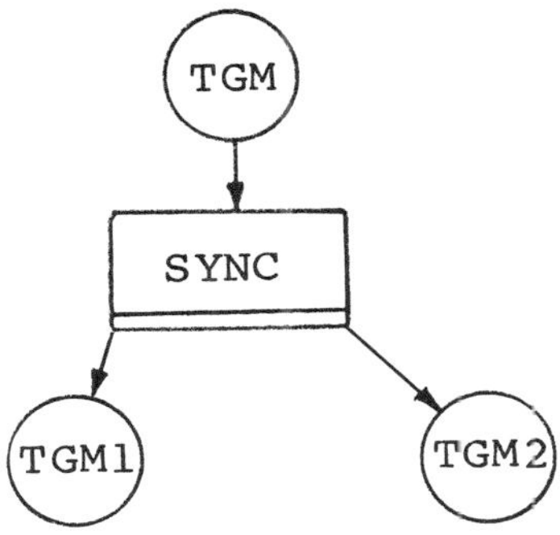

The process SYNC reads a TGM stream labelled TGM
and writes two TGM streams labelled TGM1 and TGM2
respectively.

In a SID (System Implementation Diagram) a
description of how the system is implemented in
terms of programs, procedures and datafiles is
provided. In addition to commonly used diagram
symbols, SID's use symbols which represent the
hardware devices used in the implementation. To
represent the implementation completely using
standard Jackson System Development transformations, the following symbols are used:

Simple Program Inversion
(i.e. incorporating a process as a subprocess of
another process):

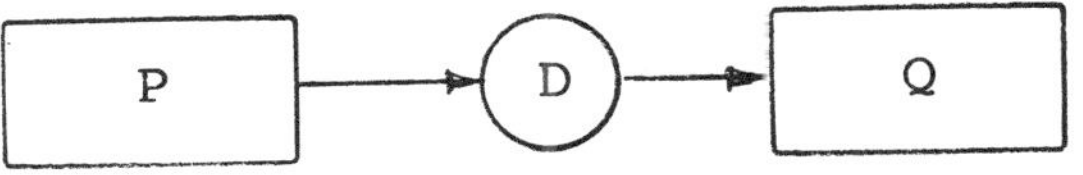

Inversion of Q with regard to D results in

(main process)

(sub process)

Inversion of P with regard to D results in

(main process)

(sub process).

State Vector Separation
(i.e. storing the state vectors, separated from
the corresponding processes, in a direct access
file):

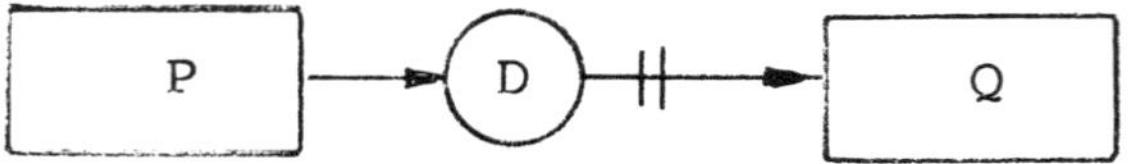

Inversion of Q with regard to D and separating
the state vector of Q results in

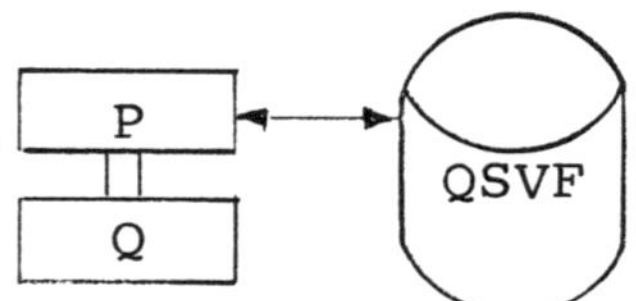

Program dismembering

If program P is dismembered (i.e. separated into
two programs which are to be treated independently), we identify the resulting programs as
P(a) and P(b).

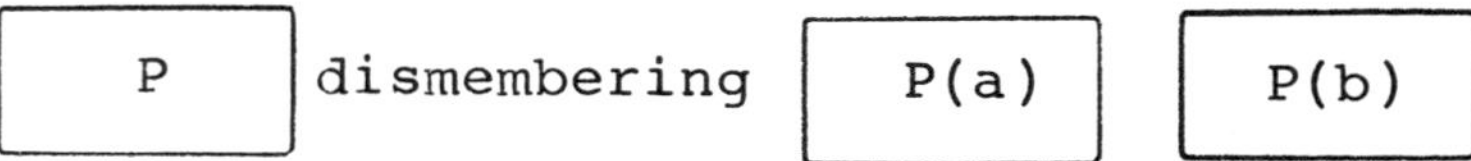

Data stream dismembering

Dismembering of a program is usually reflected in
the data stream. As a result, the following modification occurs:

is dismembered into

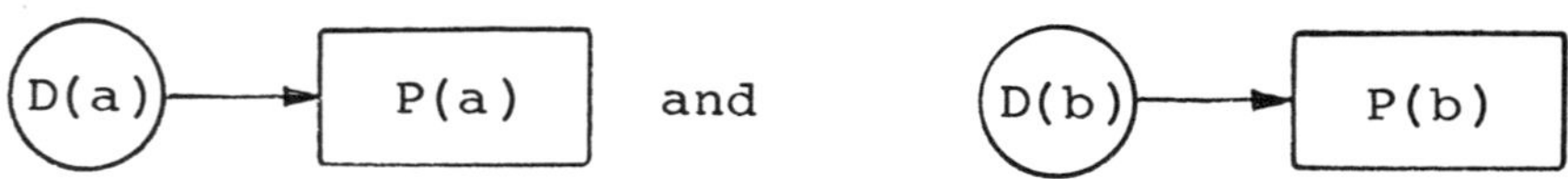

Scheduling Programs

Scheduling programs are represented by the symbol

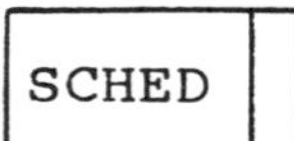

Channel Connection

When a program is connected to another which calls it by a channel (i.e. it has been inverted with regard to all of its data streams and the calling program is responsible for correct matching of the interface) the folowing notation is used

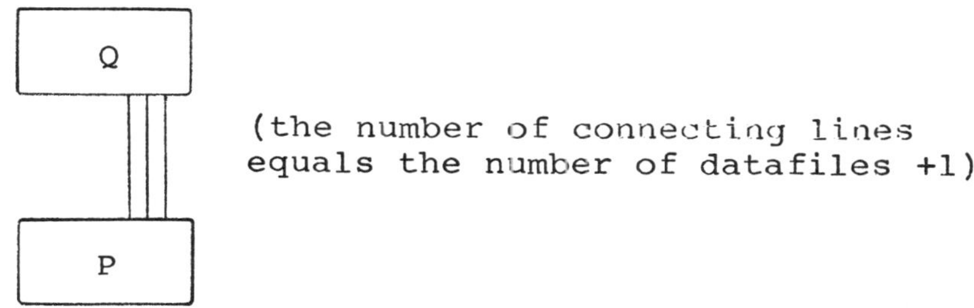

(the number of connecting lines equals the number of datafiles +1)

It is the implementation of

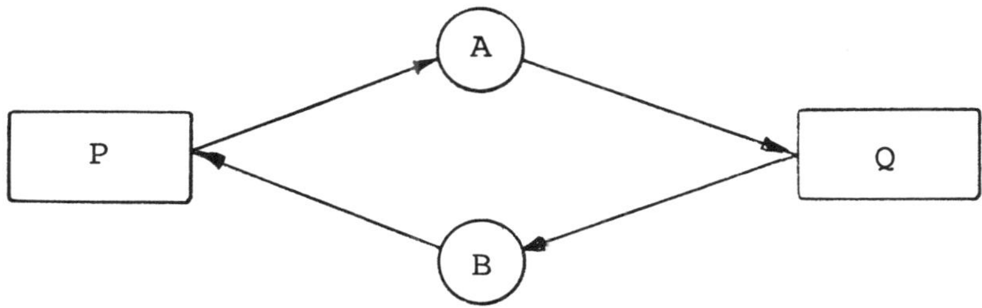

when P has been inverted with regard to A and B and Q is responsible for interface matching.

.1.4. Project management method.

No project management method is provided by the Jackson System Development Methodology. It is claimed however that most project management methods can support the methodology due to the fact that the design process has been separated into many steps.

.2. <u>Evaluation-matrix Jackson.</u>

		philosophy	working procedure	documentation method			project-management method
				tech	org	cont	
Company analysis/ synthesis	1.1						
	1.2						
	1.3						
project-selection							
Logical design	3.1						
	3.2						
Logical → technical	4.1						
	4.2						
Technical design	5.1						
	5.2						
Physical design	6.1						
	6.2						
	6.3						
	6.4						
implemen-tation							
exploita-tion							

.3. Applicability of the methodology.

.3.1. Description of the matrix coverage.

Since the Jackson methodology does not follow the classical steps for systems design, only an approximate matching with the evaluation matrix categories is possible. As stated previously, the methodology does not cover the first two phases of the evaluation matrix. It assumes that the problem area in which the method is to be used has already been defined. This probably is a result of the fact that the methodology is geared towards entities as found in the real world. It does not explicitly address the problem of data structuring as such. However, it does provide the basic information necessary to design data structures. The only explicit reference to data structuring possibilities is that state vectors may be converted to database records. However, no guidelines as to how this could be achieved are given. Nor are there any procedures given for the solution to problems which could result from the fact that the same data elements may occur in several entities.

Although the methodology also claims to cover the operational phase, (including maintenance etc.), this claim is only partly true.
Admittedly, complete documentation of the implemented system is available. And of course, it is a strong point that the system has its foundations on the "initial model" rather than on an evolving function model. But due to the number of transformations applied on the logical model to construct the implementation model, the effects of modifications in the function model are not always easily traceable
Nevertheless, the fact that the transformations are explicitly performed is a strong point in favor of this methodology.

.3.2. Thoroughness of the methodology.

The methodology is primarily geared towards process description and process interconnection. The procedure for the development of a good function model, which includes scheduling and timing features, is clearly described. However, there is a lack of an equivalent procedure for the development of the data model. Despite the statement that an entity model which handles life-cycle aspects is superior to a "classical" data model, the lack of a thorough procedure for the development of such a model is a drawback in the methodology.

.3.3.   Row transition.

Essentially one set of documentation tools is available throughout the whole design process. This guarantees a good transferability of results between the different design phases. Moreover, there is a logical transfer of results between the phases: in each design phase some new elements are added to the existing results, and sometimes an iteration is required. It is felt that the combination of using the same symbols throughout the design process, extending the set of symbols in each phase, plus a good and clear phasing of the design process allows for a good connection between the rows.

.3.4.   Column coordination.

In the design process, the working documents are essentially the same as the final documents. This ensures that the final documentation is indeed the most complete and up to date documentation. However an adequate organisation has to be built to keep track of all the documents that are produced during the design process and to check the consistency between the documents. Unfortunately, these remarks are applicable to any non-computerized documentation tool.

.4.   Observations.

As mentioned previously this methodology scores well with regard to process modelling but lacks comparable techniques for data modelling. Timing and scheduling problems are also handled well. Transformation of the logical model to the implementation model is a clear process in itself. Documentation is adequate and rather complete.

Some problems inherent in the methodology are not
discussed in the documentation. These include not
only the problems concerning data modelling but
also some rather fundamental problems in the
early stages of the design process. E.g. during
the initial model step, in which the processes
are bound together by data streams and state
vector inspection, an assumption about connections is implicitly made.
This assumption is that all "indirect" actions
(i.e. actions generated by the entity structure
which "suffers" the first action) have been
recognized in the previous modelling step as
legitimate actions. If any indirect action has
not been foreseen, one has to adapt the corresponding entity structure or insert an artificial
intermediate structure. Neither solution is desirable and both are in fact in conflict with the
basic ideas of the methodology itself.

So far, no project has been run in the Netherlands applying the Jackson System Development
methodology. This is due to the fact that this
methodology has only very recently become available. Some projects using the methodology are
being run in the U.K. The experience gained in
these projects will no doubt have its influence
on further development of the methodology. A
problem in evaluating and describing the methodology, was the almost total lack of publicly
available documentation. Through discussions with
the Dutch organisation responsible for the distribution of the methodology in the Netherlands
(RAET) some information was obtained. It is
expected that adequate documentation will soon
be publicly available.

190

References

1.   - "Program Design Techniques" EDP Analyzer, March 1979. Vol 17 no.3.

2. Jayne B. Menard - "Exxon's Experience with the Michael Jackson Design Method", Proceeding Application Development Symposium, Monterey, CA, USA, October 14-17 1979.

3. Michael Jackson - Jackson System Development, book to be published under this or a similar title May 1982. Academic Press.

4. Michael Jackson Systems Ltd. - JSD Tutorial, 1981.

3.10 PSL/PSA (Problem Statement Language/
Problem Statement Analyzer)

1. Outline of the methodology

1.1. Philosophy

The following statements should be considered as a personal view of the facts and figures presented in the PSL/PSA outlines. This means that there may well be a difference between the opinions expressed in this paper and those expressed, for example, in the original PSL/PSA documentation manuals or in the vales literature.
The PSL/PSA principles actually originate from the very ambitious objectives defined in the early phases of the ISDOS project (ref 1). These objectives were not quite obtained.

The basic rules behind ISDOS can be represented schematically as follows:

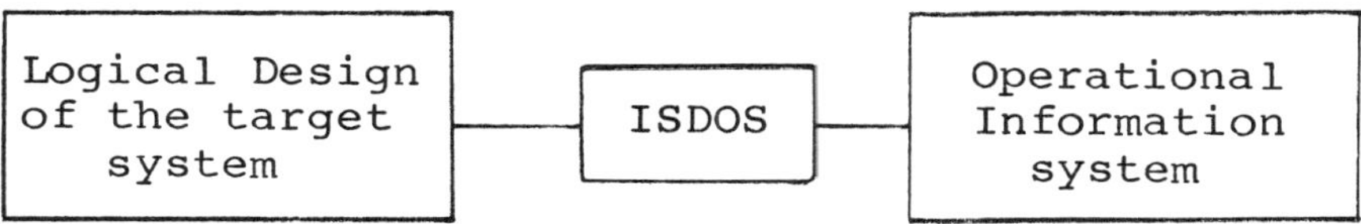

In other words, ISDOS accepts a logical systems design as input from a user (designer) and generates a completely designed (operational) information system as an output.

Even though the philosophy has been in existence for about 12 to 14 years, and despite todays state-of-the art technology, these objectives still seem overly ambitious. Many of the problems encountered during this period are still unsolved. Because of this, the ISDOS objectives have been modified. Nevertheless the resulting PSL/PSA product still offers more than any other documentation system on the market. Other documentation systems, which are generally known as Data Dictionary/Directory Systems (DD/DS), often claim to provide design aid features which, in reality do not meet the stated objectives. The PSL/PSA product, however, actually does present the systems designer with a tool which can be used not only in documentation mode (passive), but also in design-aid mode (active). To achieve this, the designer first describes the information system using the Problem Statement Language (PSL). The Problem Statement Analyzer (PSA) part of the tool then stores this information in a PSA database using its own database management system (ADBMS). The designer can then use this database as an active design-aid via a set of reporting and enquiring facilities supplied as part of the PSL/PSA system.

Because PSL/PSA is only a tool, the basic principles of the design methodology to be used in conjunction with PSL/PSA must be established at the start of the project. In this way PSL/PSA can be used as an automated documentation and design-aid geared towards the particular systems design methodology in use.

This means that the following types of questions must be answered before the start of any project activities:
   -which design methodology is to be used?
   -what documentation is required?
   -will PSL/PSA be able to cover these documentation requirements? If it cannot cover them directly, is there an alternative form of documentation within PSL/PSA which, although perhaps not optimal, will do the job?
   -do the systems designers know how to define their own "creative" products with PSL/PSA?
   -are the objectives of the design method and the documentation method clearly defined?
   -which activities should be assigned to which method?

Such questions as these, and indeed many others, generally arise whenever a DD/DS is used in the systems design process. The "management-use mode" (4) of PSL/PSA can supply the necessary DD/DS facilities.

It is necessary to introduce this idea of comparing PSL/PSA to DD/DS for the following reasons:

   1. Some DD/DS's claim to provide certain features and definition facilities which overlap with the facilities provided by PSL/PSA.

   2. Despite the fact that it has not been de-

signed to provide specific DD/DS functions, PSL/PSA offers so many parameter controlled software facilities that it lends itself naturally to use as a DD/DS.

Although it is possible then to use PSL/PSA as a DD/DS, it must be stated that there are some users who do not store any metadata at all in the PSA database, but use it only to store the actual application system data values. These users, therefore, use PSL/PSA as a Database Management System. Moreover, they use the PSA facilities as a database query and reporting system. This type of usage can also be controlled by the above mentioned parameter facilities of PSL/PSA. The fact that it is flexible enough to accomodate both forms of usage means that it is possible to customize PSL/PSA towards any required documentation objective.

This "customizing" can be done by use of the following PSL/PSA object types:

Data-oriented:	Process-oriented:
ATTRIBUTE	PROCESS
ELEMENT	PROCESSOR
GROUP	
ENTITY	
SET	
INPUT	
OUTPUT	
INTERFACE	

Dynamics-oriented:	Relationship-oriented
CONDITION	RELATION
EVENT	
TRIGGER	

One or more attributes per object type can be defined. From version 5.1 onwards, these attributes themselves may also be defined separately as object types. The "ATTRIBUTES ARE" statement, used in conjunction with the variety of object types shown, means that PSL/PSA can be applied in many different application system environments.

This ability to adapt to such a wide range of application environments is a feature which is hidden in the PSL/PSA philosophy. It is accomplished by use of an extremely comprehensive and flexible parameterized input-output structure.

1.2   Working procedure

In chapter 1.1, it was noted that a user can manipulate the many parameters available within PSL/PSA in order to create his own "customized" documentation system.

This facility can cause its own problems. In certain extreme cases, the user requirements mesh awkwardly with PSL/PSA's own predefined object types. F.e. a CODASYL schema/subschema definition done with PSL, and stored in the PSA meta-database, may cause insolvable problems. Experience obtained herewith during a workshop at the University of Michigan (where the ISDOS project is being run) shows that, before any "customizing" is done, it is necessary to have a thorough understanding of the documentation system structure (in this case of the DD/DS in use);. When this is understood, the PSL rules and options may be used to construct an integrated documentation system which will meet the user's objectives.

In order to do this, the user needs to be very familiar with all the PSL statements. The precise effect of each statement must be understood, as should the range and appearance of the PSA "outputs". The layout and the object type content of these "outputs" can also be changed by means of parameterized PSA commands. During the workshop, the following working procedure for the use of PSL/PSA as a DD/DS was used:

1. Define the entities for the metadata as required for the systems to be described, documented or registered.

2. Define the relationships between these entities.

3. Assign the attributes in the DD/DS.
   Note: In this case, all the keys and attri-

butes of the DD/DS itself were used to design a database structure beforehand. To do this, bubble-charting methodology was used. Codd's normalization rules would also lead to the required DB structure of the DD/DS

4. Divide the entities in the DD/DS into data-oriented, process-oriented, relationship-oriented and system-dynamics oriented entities.

5. Search for the attributes (or properties) of the PSL object types which approximate as closely as possible to the required DD/DS entities. This should be done whilst taking into account the general classification categories of data, process, dynamic, and relationship oriented object types.
   Note: The object type "ENTITY" as defined in PSL/PSA does not always correspond to an entity as defined in the DD/DS's mentioned in 1 to 4.

6. If the existing PSL attributes are not sufficient to describe the object types chosen, the list of attributes can be completed by use of the following PSL statement:
       ATTRIBUTES ARE attribute name(s)
   Two possibilities are available here:
     - the ATTRIBUTES ARE statement can be used within this object type.
     - the ATTRIBUTES itself may be defined as an object type. The appropriate relationship statement (within the ATTRIBUTE object type) can then be used to define for which object-occurrences this attribute will be valid.

7. After this, the output reports can be customized by means of the parameters available. This customizing must remain within the report system framework.
   Note: Some information entries are only included in certain reports on condition that necessary PSL statements are supplied. This seems obvious, but some users expect to take advantage of the full range of the PSA reporting facilities without being prepared to

196

supply the necessary input.

8. From the very beginning of the project, the user(s) must know which facilities/features or PSL statements can or should be used in which phases of the project development cycle. After these statements have been chosen, a thorough check should be made on the range of outputs which these statements make possible. The aim here is to ensure that the PSL statements chosen can be used either as a support tool for the project phase in question, or as a documentation tool to record the results.

9. If the objective is also to use PSL/PSA in the so-called "computer-use-mode" as a DD/DS, then, as a minimum, the feature of record and/or FD (file description) definition generation should be included.

    The author of this report provided the requirement for this PSL/PSA software enhancement to the ISDOS developers, and tested the updated system when the changes were incorporated. Since September 1979, the required routines have been implemented and can be activated by a normal PSA command (i.e. FDD). When using the FDD feature, certain special conditions apply to the PSL statements used. Refer to the FDD report for details.

10. For schema/subschema definition and generation, the procedure is the same as in 9.
    <u>Note</u>: This facility is not available in PSL-/PSA, but since October 1981, schema/-subschema definitions have been provided in the successor to PSL/PSA i.e. in SEM/GA (System Encyclopedia Manager/Generalised Analyser). Under SEM/GA, it is now a simple matter to describe the schema/subschema or language requirements in the SEM language ISLDS. Any desirable systems definition language or method can then be generated and stored in a central project DD/DS. This language is then available for description of the user requirements.

1.3 Documentation method

The output facilities of PSL/PSA are very powerful. Experience of this was gained during the
workshop mentioned previously. The main aim in
the workshop was to define a DD/DS. In doing
this, a rigorous separation was maintained between the logical design of a user application
system and the subsequent physical design.

It was found that, especially during the logical
design phases, the PSL/PSA system provides very
useful documentation. The documentation produced
enables the user to build up a logical design
step-by-step without being influenced by any computer oriented design considerations. The physical design stage may have an iterative impact on
the logical design because of requirements
changes, technical restrictions etc. Any changes
can easily be communicated to the user by means
of the PSL/PSA report facilities.

> Note: The process of combining and rear-
> ranging object types via relation-
> ships and other types of statements
> helps to spotlight many previously
> ill-defined or unanticipated design
> problem areas. This is, in fact, the
> manner in which PSA can best be used
> as a design aid. Other reports which
> function as design aids are based on
> techniques such as cluster analysis,
> statistical use of lower level compo-
> nents, path analysis etc.

1.4 Project management method.

In the previously mentioned workshop, in which
PSL/PSA was used as a tool to aid in the design
of a DD/DS, the project phases were successfully
structured according to SDM (Systems Development
Methodology). However, it would seem to be just
as practical to use other methods such as ARDI,
BISADA, POST etc. (their use, in conjunction with
PSL/PSA has not, however, been extensively
verified). Whichever project management method is
chosen, the conditions outlined in 1.2 point 8
must be adhered to.

.2. <u>Evaluation-matrix PSL/PSA.</u>

		philosophy	working procedure	documentationmethod			project-management method
				tech	org	cont	
Company analysis/ synthesis	1.1			////	////	////	
	1.2			////	////	////	
	1.3			////	////	////	
project-selection							
Logical design	3.1			////	////	////	
	3.2			////	////	////	
Logical → technical	4.1			////	////	////	
	4.2			////	////	////	
Technical design	5.1			////	////	////	
	5.2			////	////	////	
Physical design	6.1			////	////	////	
	6.2			////	////	////	
	6.3			////	////	////	
	6.4			////	////	////	
implementation				////	////	////	
exploitation				////	////	////	

3.   Applicability of the method

3.1   Description of the matrix coverage

The evaluation matrix suggests that PSL/PSA is primarily applicable in the documentation area. However the high degree of interaction between the documentation method of PSL/PSA and the working procedure of any chosen systems design methodology makes it difficult to describe PSL/PSA as a tool which is only used for documentation. For example, PSL/PSA can also be used as a design aid. In this, and other, respects the flexibility of PSL/PSA software is an advantage. However, this flexibility which is obtained by allowing nearly all aspects of PSL/PSA to be parameterized, can also bring disadvantages.

For example, the object type ENTITY of PSL is used in the sense of record type in the DD/DS. It may be the case that the data elements within the record type must be defined in a specific order. This is done at initial load time simply by inputting the data elements in the correct order. It is not normally possible to insert new data elements into the middle of the initial sequence. PSL/PSA is flexible enough to allow such an addition of a data element to take place. However, in order to do this, dangerous tricks which violate information integrity concepts must be performed. It would be possible to give other examples of this nature. This clearly indicates that PSL/PSA may well impact other columns of the evaluation matrix.

3.2   Thoroughness of the methodology

From the literature, it can be seen that PSL/PSA bases its intrinsic design methodology and approach on ideas derived from HIPO. It differs from HIPO in that it allows the results of precedence techniques and methodologies to be stored within the PSL/PSA structure. Another difference to HIPO is that it supports an iterative systems design approach.

As a supporting methodology, PSL/PSA seems to favor top-down systems design approaches. This does not mean that bottom-up approaches are excluded. If PSL/PSA is used purely as a documentation tool, it can also accommodate the methodology advocated by the Swedish school (Langefors et al.). This match raises the problem of dissimilar object types (ref. 1.2 points 6 and 8).

<u>Note</u>: It should also be stated that the ability to define a great varity of relationship types between object types, means that, in practice, any systems design approach can be defined and stored in PSL/PSA.

3.3   Row transition.

The connections between rows of the evaluation matrix must be considered in relation to how the PSL/PSA tool is used i.e. the inputs and outputs that it is expected to handle. If PSL/PSA is used purely as an overall design methodology, without any complementary aids, it soon becomes clear that the output is HIPO oriented. This is especially true of the early releases. This output is not at all sophisticated when compared to data and process oriented systems design methodologies.

PSL/PSA is of only limited use as a structuring and documentation tool in the physical design stages of the systems development cycle. This leads to the conclusion that a complementary design method should be used alongside PSL/PSA. However, if the minimum (and maximum) documentation requirements per project phase are established in advance and defined to PSL/PSA (as in .1.2), then connections between rows are easy to establish. Whether or not these documentation requirements are defined depends largely on the innovative forces at work in the user environment. The design aid facilities of PSL/PSA can be used as a "glue" for all complementary methodologies that wish to use the documentation possibilities of PSL/PSA.

The preceding discussion may give the impression that PSL/PSA can do everything. In one sense it can, but it may require a considerable amount of effort on the part of the user to adapt the PSL/PSA object types to meet a particular methodology or environment. It is felt that this is inevitable in any package which attempts to

handle practical situations. Many packages on the
market are too theoretical to be applied in practice, and no current package can handle every
conceivable practical case.

Note: Users who insist that the language provided
should be able to express all their objectives, without requiring any adaptation at
all, will be pleased to hear of a new
development in the ISDOS project. A meta-
language within SEM (System Encyclopedia
Manager) has been developed and this language caters for the definition of any conceivable object type or relationship type.

The output side of PSL/PSA, which is
handled by GA (Generalized Analyser) may,
however, cause problems. GA may not handle
the standard reports required by certain
languages or methodologies. In this case,
even though the metalanguage may handle the
input side adequately, the overall result
may not be satisfactory. This output problem is currently being tackled using the
many options and parameters available
within PSL/PSA.

In fact, many new software developments are
coming from the ISDOS project. If there is
sufficient user interest, new facilities
are added very quickly. For example, in
October of 1981, the CODASYL model was
generated under SEM/GA. Despite the diffi-
culties posed by the schema/subschema DDL
and DML, the whole exercise was completed
in two weeks.

3.4 Column coordination.

If PSL/PSA usage is confined to the documentation
column, then no column interaction problem exists
If, on the other hand, PSL/PSA is used in a broader context (as in the ISDOS project), then column interaction should be examined more closely.
The interfacing of PSL/PSA to other complementary
methodologies has been discussed in 2.3.

Note: This report was written from the point of
view of using PSL/PSA to design a DD/DS.
This meant that the boundaries of the documentation method column were not crossed

and that column interaction was not considered.

4. Observations.

4.1 Interfaces to other design/analysis methodologies

PSL/PSA clearly belongs to the family of hierarchical design methodologies (top-down, bottom-up) It is perhaps closest to the HIPO methodology.

This means that the output produced by PSL/PSA can easily be matched to the requirements of the philopsophy and working procedure of these hierarchical methodologies.

Note: In fact, release 5.2 of the ISDOS project now supports a network approach.

If PSL/PSA is used purely as a documentation facility, then it is capable of supporting even the "precedence and network" oriented design methods. This use as purely a documentation tool, however, goes against the philosophy and working procedures of the ISDOS design team.

4.2 Documentation.

The PSL/PSA system documentation is distributed via tape. New developments are announced and distributed on a regular basis. Efficient use of the documentation on this tape requires a certain amount of experience. It is, for example, often difficult for the user to establish what documentation is relevant to which version or release of PSL/PSA.

The availability of documentation also varies depending on the hardware/software combination on which PSL/PSA is installed. Approximately 16 different hardware/software combinations are supported. It has been observed that the PSL/PSA documentation, support, performance etc. on IBM machines seems to be of higher quality than that available on other machines.

4.3 META language

Perhaps the most important requirement of a methodology is that the documentation is generated automatically from the working procedures.

The definition language of PSL/PSA has sufficient descriptive power to be able to support this requirement for most analysis/design methodologies. The problem is that, if PSL/PSA is to fully support the working procedure of a particular methodology, the user must generate the required methodology-dependent definitions in the PSA database. Since the demands of PSL/PSA may be considered as secondary to the demands of the design methodology, users may not always take time to generate these definitions.

This, in fact, is the main issue behind the development of the META language mentioned in 3.3.

With META, all the necessary object types required by means of the ISLDS language, and then added to a meta definition library. From this point onwards, documentation of the analysis results and of the information systems to be constructed, can be done by PSL/PSA in the language of the target design methodology.

Release of a graphical input/output feature (Graphics Interface) is also planned. This feature will allow the user to describe an informaton system in terms of the graphical symbols used in many methodologies.

One final remark is that, where META/GA is used, only one DD/DS is needed to second the information required by all methodologies used in the system development cycle. This is an important feature because it is often necessary to use tools from 3 or 4 different methodologies in the systems development process. Once the methodologies are described in the META system, GA can be used to generate the user manuals for each methodology from the DD/DS database. If this feature was not available, each design methodology would require its own documentation database.

As with PSL/PSA, META/GA can also be installed on many different hardware/software configurations.

References.

1) Elsenaar, A.

PSL/PSA een hulpmiddel bij het ontwikkelen van informatiesystemen, Informatie, jaargang 21 nr.5, pp.282-348

2) Teichroew, D.
   Sayani, H.

Automation of system building, Datamation, August 15, 1971, pp.2503

3)

PSL/PSA manuals

4) Janssen, T.G.M.
   Gersteling, H.
   Peeters, J.

Data Dictionaries/Directories, Informatie,jaargang 20, oktober 1978

5) Bernus, P.
   Havatny, J.

Computer Aids to the Design of Integrated Manufacturing Systems, Computers in Industry I, (1979) 11-19, North Holland Publ. Co.

6) Martin Tulic

Getting Ready for Structured Analysis, Proceedings, Application Development Symposium, Monterey, California, October 14-17, 1979, pp.187-202

Chapter 4   The Evaluation Matrix

4.1. Description of the classification

Chapter 1 and 2 introduced the evaluation matrix developed by Thunnissen. This matrix was used to classify and to compare the methods and techniques studied.
Each methodology was examined from the four viewpoints of: the philosophy, the working procedure, the documentation method and the project management method. The division into phases is explained in 4.1.2. One extra phase has been added to Thunnissen's original matrix. This is the company analysis-synthesis which precedes project selection. It has been added because it appears that, in most cases, there is no formal method for evaluating anticipated project benefits from an integral company viewpoint before project selection takes place.

4.1.1. The horizontal axis

The divisions on the horizontal axis are for:
1- The <u>philosophy</u> on which the methodology is based. This philosophy must explain the theoretical principles on which the practical techniques are based. It must give practical, useable definitions of the terms and symbols used in the methodology (e.g. of terms such as 'process', 'data', information system' etc.), and it must explain how to recognise the abstract phenomena it describes in the real world (e.g. it must say what criteria are used to recognise such things as a 'process' etc.). The philosophy should also give a formal definition of any languages it uses e.g. a 'process definition language'. Other points which should be explained by the philosophy are, for example:
   - is the working procedure based on a top-down, bottum up or some other approach?
   - is it oriented towards data or towards processes?

206

2- <u>The working procedure</u>, which describes the way
the philosophy is translated into a set of
practical tools which assist in the analysis,
design and implementation of information systems.
The working procedure should say which tools
are relevant to which phases of the systems
development cycle e.g. to the analysis of the
company as a whole, to process and/or data
analysis, to systems design, to programming,
to implementation and to evaluation after
implementation. Guidelines must also be given
as to how much effort is to be expended on
each project phase, and when work for a
particular phase can be considered complete.
Clear, formal definitions of things such as:
'process definition language','data definition
language', structuring rules, schema techniques etc. become essential here, because
these are the tools which the analyst must
understand and use to achieve his objectives.

3- <u>The documentation method</u> describes the contents of the documentation to be produced, and
at what stage of the development cycle each
document should be produced. It should also
say how the documentation is to be organised.
Each document must be fully described. Practical guidelines and clarifying examples
should also be given for each form described.
Ideally, all relevant documentation should be
produced whilst the project activities concerned are actually being performed.
In summary the documentation method must give
guidelines for:
- <u>what documentation</u> is to be produced at what
  <u>stage</u>
- a description of the <u>contents</u>
- <u>what techniques</u> should be used to produce
  the documentation (e.g. modelling techniques, or usage of forms)
- how the documentation is to be organised
  (e.g. centrally or decentrally; how is it
  classified?; what codes are used?; how is it
  retrieved?; who should read it?).

It is clear that the working procedure, which
describes what is to be done in each phase,
and the documentation procedure, which des-

cribes what is to be produced in each phase, are closely related to the project management method.

4- <u>The project management method</u> is a description of how the various elements of the methodology are to be organised to achieve the aims in a project environment.

The project management method must give guidelines for: project organisation; division into phases; activities per phase; milestones; responsibilities; interface to the company's organisational structure; budgetary provisions necessary at each phase etc. It should also describe any specific technique to be used for planning or for cost/benefit analysis.

All phases on the project wheel of the systems bi-cycle (chapter 2) must be covered by the project management method. In addition, this method must provide a 'signal translation mechanism', which can receive and interpret signals from the process wheel of the systems bicycle, and an 'implementation mechanism' which shows how the project 'product' is to be integrated into the company business processes.
To achieve these aims, the project management method must be closely tuned to the philosophy, working procedure and documentation method of the methodology concerned.

<u>4.1.2. The vertical axis.</u>

As stated previously, the divisions chosen here are subjective, but they can easily be compared to the divisions advocated by most methodologies currently in use.

- <u>the company analysis/synthesis</u> which aims at building a model, or models, to describe how the company functions in a business environment (see chapter 2). This analysis/synthesis can be divided into three tasks:
  1. integral analysis/synthesis of company processes, resulting in an overall process structure model (1.1)

    2. integral analysis/synthesis of the company data resulting in an overall data structure model (1.2)

    3. description of the company model in which both data and processes are included. This description could take the form of an information/automation plan.

Although a distinction is made here between process and data analysis, one should bear in mind that this is done only to aid in evaluating and classifying different aspects of the methodologies in question. In practice, there is a high degree of interaction between both analytical techniques.

- <u>the project selection</u> is performed on the basis of the results of the company analysis/synthesis. In this project selection procedure, priorities are allocated both to projects already in progress as well as to proposed future projects. These projects deal with the resolution of problems encountered in the business functions of the company. The business processes involved, and the anticipated project 'product', must be clearly defined.

Final project selection is based on the priorities allocated, the budget provided and the availability of other required company resources.

- <u>the logical design</u> carries the analysis/-synthesis of the company's data and processes to a more detailed level. The resulting 'logical design' consists of the detailed process and data models (see 3.1 and 3.2).
In this step, the impact of the logical systems design on current and future organisational structures should be taken into account.

- <u>the transformation</u> from logical to technical design. This step synthesises outputs of the previous phases resulting in the production of a requirements model. It is the job of subsequent phases to satisfy the requirements specified in this model.
A separation is made between the mappings of:

a. from logical systems design (process model) to technical systems design (4.1)
b. from logical data structure (data model) to technical file design (4.2)

This step was proposed by Thunnissen and is considered essential in order to perform the transformation from logical to technical design (mapping). Most methodologies do not support this step. This transformation involves an effort which is often underestimated. It is therefor included explicitly as a separate phase in the matrix.

- <u>the technical design</u> consists of:
  - the technical system design (5.1)
  - the technical file design   (5.2)

- <u>the physical design</u> includes construction of:
  -programs (application construction) (6.1)
  -detailed user procedures   (6.2)
  -computer centre procedures   (6.3)
  -files (file construction)   (6.4)

- <u>the implementation</u> of the automated information system. This includes acceptance and conversion procedures.

- <u>the operation</u> of the system. This includes provisions for evaluation and maintenance of the system.

This division into steps outlined above has been thoroughly discussed. However, it is recognised that it is possible to divide methodology cycles into different divisional categories. The division chosen seems to us to be those most suited to the evaluation of current systems development methodologies.

4.2 Findings.

4.2.1 Company analysis/synthesis and project selection.

Only IBM's BSP methodology deals explicitly with the phases of company analysis/synthesis and project selection. This methodology gives both corporate and DP management an insight into the functioning of the company in terms of processes, information flows, data classes and related organisational units.

Methods such as ISAC, SASO, MOS, SADT, NIAM and BC could be used in the company analysis/-synthesis phase in order to describe the overall process structures and information flows. However, none of these methodologies address organisational, personnel and financial aspects on the strategic level, and it is felt that there is a need for special management oriented tools in these areas. ISAC, SASO and MOS aim especially at analysis of the information flows connecting processes. They also show how the information processes relate to the business activities of the object system. NIAM and BC focus on the logical structure of the data. NIAM in particular uses the 'role concept' to relate data to processes in a 'static' manner. The BC technique is often used in conjunction with James Martin's relationship matrices to show the connection between data, processes and organisational units. SADT is the only methodology that uses one diagrammatic technique (see the four-sided box) to show both process and data structures.

As far as the four horizontal axis viewpoints are concerned, BSP describes its basic philosophy well and now supplies adequate definitions of terms such as business processes, data classes, etc. It also gives examples to show how these abstract concepts can be identified in practice.

BSP gives a suitable description of what steps are to be performed, what documentation is to be produced. It does not include any techniques for the organisation of this documentation, nor does it supply any automated documentation tools. Most elements for project management are supplied. So it should be a relatively easy matter to use BSP in combination with other standard project management tools.

As stated in chapter 2, project selection is not explicitly identified as being of prime concern to the company management. BSP does provide rules for project selection, whereas most methodologies simply leave this task to the user management.

4.2.2.Logical design.

The degree to which the methodologies studied covered this phase, and subsequent matrix phases, was the subject of much animated discussion within the study team. Several proposals were discussed and regarded before final agreement was reached.

a. working procedure and philosophy.

Detailed process analysis.
Both MOS and SASO lean towards the ISAC 'Scandinavian school'.The ISAC method relates outputs to inputs by means of transformation processes.These processes are represented on the diagrams by dots, and each dot is given a process (activity) name.In other words, the methodology makes it clear that processes exist to transform input into output, but it does not attempt to describe the internal logic of the processes at this stage. This type of methodology is, in principle information or data oriented, as opposed to being process oriented.

SASO mentions the independent procedure as an important concept for information system structuring. Both SASO and MOS use the elementary process as a basic building block on the lowest level.
SADT and NIAM favor a process oriented philosophy. SADT uses a four-sided box notation technique wich differs considerably from the technique used in the other methodologies.
This technique is applied, within SADT, to both process and data analysis. NIAM uses information flow diagrams (IFD's) and starts with the primary company processes.
Jackson's Structured Design also includes a detailed process analysis resulting in a process model. Its angle of approach however, differs very much from the other methodologies mentioned so far. The basic idea behind Jackson's structured Design is the life-history approach towards systems design. This implies, that of each entity (type) a life cycle is determined including the processes that may be performed on the entity (occurrence) in its entire existence. This results in a process model relating all entity (types) on the basis of

interconnected life histories. The approach is somewhat similar (though less formal) to the Abstract Data Type (ADT)-approach.

The working procedure is, in all cases (with the possible exception of Jackson), based upon a top-down decomposition of rough input/output descriptions into more detailed descriptions. The procedures differ from methodology to methodology because of the emphasis placed on different activities, and the sequence in which these activities are to be carried out (see chapter 3).

<u>Detailed data analysis</u> which results in a 'data model' is supported by SASO, MOS, SADT, NIAM and BC (in its philosophy). SASO bases data analysis on the outputs from the precedence analysis. It uses a bottom-up approach, starting with, for example, an aggregration of data (cf. C.J. Date), and ending with normalised data structures as described by Codd. The detailed process analysis of SASO, which shows 'how' the data are transformed, also uses a bottum-up approach starting at the lowest level of information analysis (by using the output from precedence analysis). SADT uses the same analysis and documentation techniques for both data and process analysis. NIAM bases data analysis on the idea of a 'conceptual model'. This model shows the data structure in terms of units known as 'roles, objects and sentences'. In its final form, NIAM's data model corresponds to a normalised data structure. NIAM uses the 'role' concept to provide a means of relating objects to processes i.e. the data model is used as the starting point for the first, or lowest level, information flow diagram (IFD).

MOS combines, in an interactive manner, a top-down data analysis approach with a precedence analysis approach.

BC starts by using information bubbles to express information units and then groups them by examining the mutual functional dependencies that exist between these data units. The BC method has much in common with the data analysis method of NIAM, and can be considered as a subset of the latter. BC techniques are also used as part of the SASO method.

b. Documentation method

The documentation method for MOS, SASO and ISAC is based on the diagrams or graphs produced (in particular, on the precedence graphs) and on the accompanying textual descriptions. These methodologies do not provide any documentation support tools.

SASO and SADT also give a documentation method for the description of processes. They describe the contents of the documentation and the techniques used to produce it, they do not provide any organisational or support tools. In the BC methodology, a documentation technique is given, but content descriptions and organisational tools are not provided.

NIAM relies on the documented information flow diagrams (IFD's) and the data models which show the relevant roles, objects and sentences.

Jackson's Structured Design supplies a full set of documentation rules to be applied to process analysis. Less abundant however are the rules to describe the resulting data models in an effective way. No automated tools are available to support the analysis process.

The PSL/PSA documentation method can, in principle, be applied to all the methodologies studied. This is because PSL/PSA provides an interface which allows the user to incorporate the terms used in the working procedure of any methodology into the PSL/PSA documentation method.

c. Project management method

Project management methods are, in general, not very advanced and none of the methodologies studied offered very sophisticated tools in this area. This is not really very surprising because:

214

- project management is primarily concerned
  with the management of such project aspects
  as, for example: cost, time taken per phase,
  availability of specialists, scheduling of
  training. Systems design methodologies are,
  on the other hand, primarily concerned with
  the quality of the system to be constructed.

- project management requirements vary greatly
  according to such things as the company
  management climate, the type of organisation
  and the finance available.

- project management is influenced by the
  project teams professional attitude and by
  the background of the project team leader and
  members (i.e. from a user organisation, or
  from the DP department).

For these reasons, one cannot expect to find
analysis and design methodologies which, even
if they cover the complete range of project
activities, are embedded in a comprehensive
project management method. In fact, given the
diversity of project management methodologies
and of systems development methodologies available, it may not be a good idea to decide on
the use of only one fixed combination of
methodologies. A better approach might be to
select the appropriate combination for a
particular project in the pre-study phase.

4.2.3.
Transformation from logical to technical design

This transformation is fully supported by SASO
and Jackson, but only partly supported by SADT,
MOS and NIAM. BC supports this transformation only on the data structuring side (see the matrices
of chapter 3).
All five of these methodologies handle this
transformation from the point of view of philosophy, working procedure and documentation. None
of them, with the possible exception of SADT,
handles it from a project management viewpoint.

4.2.4. Technical design

Technical systems design, in the sense of process structuring, is supported by ISAC, Jackson, SASO and partly by MOS. NIAM only supports the technical data structure design. The philosophy, working procedure and documentation method of all these methodologies cover the phase of technical design. Only SADT covers it from a project management viewpoint.

4.2.5. Physical design

Physical design is partially supported by NIAM and SASO. ISAC supplies tools for the description of the detailed user procedures.
Jackson supports this phase with respect to program structuring using pseudo-code. No rules are given explicity however for physical file design.

4.2.6. Implementation

Implementation is not supported by any of the methodologies studied.

4.2.7. Operation

This phase too is not supported by any of the methodologies studied.

Chapter 5. Conclusions and recommendations.

5.1 Summary of the evaluation matrix coverage.

This summary considers the degree to which the methodologies studied cover the different blocks of the evaluation matrix.

- Of all the methodologies, only BSP deals explicitly with company analysis/synthesis and project selection. The other methodologies should pay further attention to these important stages.

- One promising development is the possible coupling of BSP and SASO techniques in order to achieve a more complete matrix coverage.
However a suitable documentation method and project management method would have to be developed for this combination to be viable.
Neither methodology, as yet, covers the task of physical design completely.
One possible difficulty to be overcome here is the problem of combining the generalized BSP approach towards information flow with the more detailed SASO approach.

- A coupling which has already been tried in practice is that of ISAC with the data analysis methodology of CACI (the latter methodology is not described in this report). This combination allows equal attention to be given to data and process analysis aspects, but care should be taken to find suitable documentation and project management methods. The phases of company analysis/synthesis and project selection are not covered, nor, at the other end of the cycle, is the physical design phase.
ISAC, nevertheless, covers many of the aspects considered by the study team, and its basic concepts have been used in developing extensions such as MOS and SASO. ISAC also handles the connections between all phases of the project cycle of the systems bi-cycle.
The MOS and SASO extensions of top-down data analysis and independent procedure definition could be used to improve ISAC.

- SADT offers interesting possibilities in the area of company analysis/synthesis. It is also

strong in that it gives equal weight to the
activities of data and process analysis. It
lacks, however, a mechanism to connect the
phase of technical design to the phase of
physical design. It also lacks an adequate
documentation method and project management
method.
The possibility of using PSL/PSA as a documentation support tool for SADT has been considered.

- The latest version of NIAM (Nijssen's methodology) incorporates an 'object-system analysis'
which resembles ISAC's activity study and
SASO's object system analysis. It also asso-
ciates the use of a hierarchy of information
flow diagrams (IFD's) to study the total
information flow. The rules for decomposition
and aggregation need to be further clarified if
they are to be of use in a practical working
situation e.g. the rules for coupling and
binding need to be clarified. A system called
ISDIS (Information Systems Development and
Implementation System) has been created to
provide data dictionary/directory support for
NIAM.

- The approach taken in Jackson's Structured
Design based on the life history of entities is
a very interesting one. It is closely related
to the approach taken in the Abstract Data
Type-approach. Statements that this approach
results, especially with regard to processes,
in a more stable process model than the 'classical' approaches, is defendable. However, it
still has to be proven in practice. It is regrettable that JSD's does not deal explicitly
with data structuring. All information to be
used in the data structuring process, is available however.

- PSL/PSA has powerful documentation support
facilities which can, in principle, be used
with any of the methodologies studied. The
structuring approaches of the target methodology must be thoroughly understood because the
concepts behind this structuring must be clearly defined in PSL/PSA. Examples of such coupling are that of SADT and PSL/PSA, which is
described in "Computers and Industry" , and of

SASO and PSL/PSA. The latest ISDOS developments aim at solving the remaining problems caused by the diversity of working procedures and documentation methods in the various methodologies with SEM/GA (System Encyclopedia Manager/Generalised Analyser).

- Warnier/Orr is primarily concerned with logical design. It appears to be extremely difficult to combine with the other necessary methodologies.

5.2. Problems in applying the methodologies.

5.2.1. Documentation of the methodologies

In general it can be said that most of the methodologies studied are not accompanied by adequate documentation. It was often necessary to gather information from outside literary sources. In most cases, the documentation can be obtained separately e.g. with BSP, ISAC, SASO, MOS, PSL/PSA and NIAM. SADT documentation must be paid for, and Jackson documentation should become available in the course of 1982.
In descriptions of the philosophy, one finds many non-standard terms and definitions which are either inadequately defined, or simply not defined at all. This seems to mirror the problems of the rapidly changing world of the computing industry itself.

5.2.2 Education and training.

The education and training offered is, in many cases, not satisfactory. Normally, the supplier or producer of the methodology will demand payment for the education or training provided. If these services are supplied for free, it is often in the hope that the client will join the methodology user group and so spread the use of the methodology more widely.
Often the approach taken is to educate and train a team of specialists by using the methodology in a 'research' project. The theoretical knowledge and practical experience is then centred in this team. The members of this team may provide support in subsequent projects which use the methodology.

5.2.3 Support.

The support often takes the form of 'on-the-job' training i.e. the supplier will put one or more consultants at the disposal of the specialist project team. These consultants work with the team and quite often appear simply to be learning the methodology along with the rest of the team. This is the case with SASO, NIAM, MOS, BSP and to a lesser extend with SADT and ISAC. Warnier/Orr and BC must be learnt from the documentation provided. The Jackson methodology tends to be supported by independent software houses. PSL/PSA is delivered in the form of a tape plus documentation, but application support can also be obtained.

5.2.4 Supporting tools.

Supporting tools for the documentation and project management methods are generally not supplied. Only PSL/PSA supplies good facilities for documentation support at a comparatively low price. These facilities are delivered in the form of a magnetic tape plus supporting programs which can be used to process the outputs of the analysis and design phases, and to ensure the consistency of the phase outputs.
BSP and NIAM claim that data dictionary support is available. At the moment, this support is restricted to IBM and CDC users rspectively. In our opinion, these data dictionary facilities support only a limited subset of the services required.

5.2.5 Ease of use for users and DP-personnel

Some suppliers claim that end-users will find the methodology easy to use. This claim appears at the present moment, to be questionable. If the methodology is to be successfully applied in practice, both users and DP-personnel must have a thorough understanding of the philosophy on which the methodology is based. For most users, however, the context in which the methodology is to be used, and the jargon used within the methodology itself, form a barrier to understanding.
NIAM starts from the idea that users should be able to handle the 'roles-objects-sentences'

concepts. In practice, it is the information analyst who uses the methodology, and different analysts do not always interpret its terms and its working procedure consistently.

The ISAC methodology is, in principle, easy to use. In practice, users sometimes have difficulty with the diagrammetic techniques and with the non-formalised decomposition rules. Essentially the same can be said of MOS, SASO and BSP.

Methods such as Jackson, Warnier/Orr, BC and PSL/PSA are, in fact, intended for use by information analysts and systems designers. Even though SADT uses the same techniques to describe processes and data, users have difficulty in using the box-notation techniques.

N.B. The ISDOS development mentioned in 5.1 may take a step towards improving the useability aspect of methodologies in general. This development offers improvements based on:
-graphical terminal and word processor support for PSL/PSA.
-the ISDOS meta-language and SEM/GA concepts.
The features will aid the user to describe requirement statements, system specifications, procedures etc. in his own terms and/or in the language of any other methodology chosen for use with PSL/PSA. Practical experience in the use of such integrated tools is, however, as yet limited.

In contrast to users, DP personnel, such as information analysts, system designers, data analysts and programmers, find it easier to integrate methodology techniques into their normal job activities. This still requires an initial education and training effort. Problems can arise if the philosophy and working procedure of the chosen methodology do not agree with the theoretical ideas and/or practical experience of the DP personnel concerned.

Another question to be answered is whether or not a particular methodology is internally consistent. If it is internally consistent, a methodology will always produce the same outputs from the same inputs. This means that, when used at different times by different teams of people, a methodology applied to the same company and/or problem area should produce the same results.

N.B. Practical experience in the use of integrated methods and techniques, sometimes using automated support tools, is growing. More experience seems to be needed if these integrated techniques are to be used in conjunction with future developments such as automated software generation and file creation.

5.2.6. Extendability of the methodologies.

This subject has not been covered explicitly in this report. Certain aspects of it have been covered when considering how it might be possible to extend some methodologies by interfacing them to other methodologies. In practice, it is important that the methodology chosen is flexible enough to accomodate changes imposed by new techniques or user desires. It should be possible to incorporate such demands without radically changing the philosophy or working procedure of the methodology. Whilst such questions depend in part on the methodology itself, much will also depend on the ability and the willingness of the supplier to respond to requests for change.

5.3. Recommendations for selection and use of a methodology

5.3.1. Selection

When selecting a methodology, a number of important factors can be isolated e.g.
- ease of use
- time necessary to learn the methodology
- the scope of the methodology (cf. the evaluation matrix coverage)
- the frame of reference (i.e. the terms and definitions used)
- the availability and accessibility of documentation
- supporting tools supplied for documentation and project management
- compatibility with current organisational practices
- the cost of education, implementation and use
- standardisation possibilities offered
- the manageability of projects with the methodo-

logy

The study team gives the following guidelines for the selection of a suitable methodology.

(a) Before making a selection, define the general requirements that a methodology must fulfil in terms of such features as: the frame of reference, methodology scope, ease of use, costs and supporting tools.
The study group used the evaluation matrix for this purpose. Although the matrix categories may be somewhat subjective, it was found to be of great help as a comparison tool.

(b) Consider the needs and abilities of all potential users of the methodology, and the phases of the project in which they intend to use it. For example, the features that user groups seek in a methodology often differ widely from those sought by DP personnel. And again, a methodology suitable for programming may be entirely inadequate to cope with higher levels in the systems development cycle.

(c) Use the results of (a) and (b) to study those methodologies which appear to satisfy the general criteria outlined. One problem here is that the criteria chosen may well reflect the special knowledge and interests of the evaluation team rather than the company as a whole. The best way to overcome this, is to circulate the criteria chosen amongst the potential user groups before the detailed study process in started.
It is best not to rely solely on the methodology documentation, but, where possible, to visit other organisations who are already using the methodology and to discuss their experiences.

(d) Evaluate the findings and select the methodology which best satifies the selection criteria outlined, and which is most suitable for the potential user groups. This is best done by 'weighting' the relevant selection criteria, and then seeing how well or badly each candidate methodology satisfies these criteria.

(e) Make sure that all people who will be invol-
     ved in the use of the methodology receive
     appropriate education and on-the-job train-
     ing. Ideally, these services are first pro-
     vided by the one supplier company, and then
     the company's own personnel can train people
     to use the methodology in subsequent phases.

5.3.2. Use

When a methodology is introduced, initial expectations are normally far too optimistic. The best
way to avoid this is to talk to other organisations who have used the methodology in a practical environment. More realistic goals for mea-
suring the success or failure of the methodology
can then be set.
Ideally, all members of the project team should
have practical experience in using the methodology. If only one person on the team is familiar
with the methodology techniques, he or she may
well impose a very subjective interpretation of
the rules on the whole project team. This is
dangerous because, if the project fails, the
methodology could unfairly be blamed.

First time users need to be supported by an
expert, and the project planning must allow for
learning-curve effect.
Essential to the success of the use of any methodology is the implementation of a good documentation method. This is crucial for the control
and management of the project, and for reporting
results to the participants and to the management
concerned.
Some sort of documentation support tool, prefe-
rably an automated tool such as a data dictionary, is necessary to control the consistency
of the analytical results. Physical management of
the documentation produced can also be aided by
the use of the word processing or terminal
editing secretarial facilities.
It is not unusual to use a new methodology in an
attempt to remove bottlenecks which may have
plagued the company for years. If, however, these
bottlenecks are caused by such factors as poor
coordination, poor communication or poor project

management, then the introduction of a methodology on its own will not solve the problems. Care
should be taken not to abandon a good methodology
because of isolated cases of bad practice.

References.

<u>Appendix 2</u>   Contents 'definitions and terms'.

<u>1. Process</u>

1.1. Process, sub (sub) process
1.2. Elementary process
1.3. Activity
1.4. Process function
1.5. Process flow

<u>2. Corporate analysis/-synthesis</u>

2.1. Process relations
3.2. Corporate model

<u>3. Process analysis (dynamic acpect)</u>

3.1. Information system (IS)
3.2. Information sub (sub) system
3.3. Elementary information system
3.4. Process model
3.5. Information system - data relation

<u>4. Data analysis (static aspect)</u>

4.1. Data structure
4.2. Data
4.3. Data element
4.4. Element type
4.5. Data relation
4.6. Information
4.7. Message, information flow

<u>5. Project.</u>

5.1. Project phasing
5.2. Project planning
5.3. Project activity
5.4. Project organisation
5.5. Project management
5.6. Project secretary
5.7. Project documentation

<u>Definitions and terms for the evaluation study.</u>

The following definitions and terms have to be seen in the light of the 'model-approach' as described in chapter 2 and the schema given in that chapter.

First a "definition" is given of each term used in the study. Subsequently under a. references are made to definitions used by others and under b. examples are given to clarify.
Not in all cases however points a. and b. have been referenced. In these cases, similar definitions lack altogether or examples would be to elaborate for the purpose of clarification.

<u>1. Process</u> = a bundling of logically rela-
ted activities as they are
manifest within a company or
organisation and as they are
executed by (groups of) people; company process.
a. function, functional area,
object system
b. salesprocess, personnel,
administration process, education process.

<u>1.1.</u>
<u>Sub</u> (sub) process = a grouping of logically rela-
ted activities, within a pro-
cess; process.
a. subfunction, functional
subarea.
b. sales control process,
personnel review process, re-
training process.

<u>1.2.</u>
<u>Elementary</u> process= a process intrinsically being
equipped with all information
to perform its aimed function
independent procedure
a. module, elementary procedure, "transaction", independent procedure
b. flight reservation,filling
in review form, instruction.

<u>1.3.</u>
<u>Activity</u> = an action for the creation,
the acquisition or the fur-
nishing of a "product"; the
logically connected activities belonging together form
an elementary process.
a. operation, "proces", (working) course, action
b. registering a persons name
filling out a particular form
show a machinehandling, field
demo.

In all process definitions, one can distinguish
between the process function and the process
flow:

<u>1.4</u>
<u>Process</u> function = the aim/goal of a process,
This aim will be shown in the
naming of the process and
will be described in the process description.
a. function, functional area.
b. sales control process has
as a goal the control of the
sales of the articles produced by a company.

<u>1.5</u>
<u>Process</u> flow = the course of the process
actions, as performed in time
and place. In the description
of the process flow the natural language can be used,
or a (to be defined) formal
language (process definition
language) with flow charts
etc.
a. "Process-Ablauf", course
of a process.

2. Corporate
   analysis/
   synthesis

= the "investigation" of all the existing processes in a company/organisation that is subject of research, also the sub (sub..) processes and the elementary processes in order to:
• describe these in natural language
• describe them in a formal language (if possible)
• relate these processes on the basis of "material flow" (goods, money etc.), if any.
•   "describe/expose"   them using elementary processes as building stones (modular building)
• record them in the 'documentation' by means of these descriptions.
with the main objective to:
• describe a corporate model in which:
  - the functioning of the whole company/organisation is reflected
  - the mutual internal/external "material flows" are recorded
  - the processes are related to the functioning (groups of) people.

a. functional specification, performance specification, specification, functional analysis.

2.1
Process relations = the "real" relations , the relations in real world that can be given as existing between processes, sub (sub..) processes, elementary processes.

These relations can refer to:
• 'material flows' between

processes etc. (for example
raw material, products,
forms, finance, material.)
- 'information streams' between processes etc. (for
example information about
the 'real stream', but also
about the functioning of
the processes)
- 'control streams' from and
to processes etc. (for
example information about
the input stream for pro-
cess A gives control-infor-
mation for the functioning
of process B. Example: the
number of people that want
to use a particular flight
can deliver control information for the process that
deals with the flight scheduling).

2.2.

Corporate model = the description of the
functioning company/organisa-
tion by means of:

- the description of the processes
- the description of the process relations (information
flows, material flows)
- the description of a company process schema (the model)

In this company model are also
mentioned the results of the
research on:

- potential bottlenecks within
processes and between processes, that may result in
bottlenecks in:

  - 'material flow' (production, goods etc.)
  - 'information flow", such as
the lack of information

about processes.
- controllability of processes
- the functioning of processes because of human fac-
tors (e.g. incomplete or
malfunctioning of people in
processes).
- process goals/aims. (incomplete, incorrect formulated
goals
- expectations with regard to
process executions and
their results (incorrect
expectation pattern);
• results that can be expected
from proposed solutions with
regard to bottlenecks, such
as:

- alternative process structure
- alternative process goals
- propositions for organisational changes
- propositions for process
changes
- propositions for (automated) information supply.

• costs and benefits to be expected from the proposed solutions (compromises, trade-
offs)

The companymodel may include an
"informationplan".

3.

Process analysis= the determination of the activities within the process.

This analysis aims at specifying which activities and which information are needed for (groups of) people and their tools within processes in order to make possible the actions of these people;the <u>dynamic aspect</u>

The analysis results in a description of the processes and sub (sub...) processes logically interrelated on the basis of the company analysis/synthesis. The result is the 'process-model'.

The goal of this analysis for the processes, sub (sub...) processes and activities is:

- to describe them in natural language
- to describe them in a formal language (if possible)
- to relate them mutually by means of the information streams to be described (dynamic aspects).
- to describe their functioning (dynamic aspect)
- to be part of a logical system development

<u>a</u> systemanalysis, systemdevelopment, (logical) system design, system specification, information analysis.

3.1.

Information system

= a complex of logically interrelated processes to support a company process

The "information image" of a process, in casu the description of a process from the information aspect using the

234

language(s) from the science of informatics.

a. system
b. informationsystem for stock control.

3.2.
Information sub = a subset of an information sys-
(sub..)system   tem. The subsystem should re-
                 flect a complex of interrela-
                 ted, recognizable company acti-
                 vities.

a. sub (sub...) system, system element, systempart.
b. informationsubsystem for stock-intake.

3.3.
Elementary   = a basic informationsubsystem
information   This elementary informationsys-
system   tem can not be subdivided into
                   meaningful sub-subsystems and
                   serves as building stone for
                   the informationsystem.

a. systemelement, component, module, systempart.
b. informationsubsystem for the intake of specific stock.

N.B. An elementary information system can possibly serve as a building stone in several information (sub) system (modular approach).

3.4.
Process model   = the ordered structure of mutu-
                   ally related informationsystems
                   to be defined on the basis of
                   the processes analysed, sub
                   (sub...) processes.

a. objectmodel, systelogical model.

3.5.
IS-data relation= the description of the relation
between information systems and
the relevant data, taking into
account the datastructure (see
4.1.).

4.
<u>Data</u> analysis = the determination and defini-
tion of the data used by the
processes and, as such relevant
to the information systems.

This research aims at:
. the unique specification of
data
. the description of the data
in the context of:
- the naming of data
- the relations between data
- the properties of data
. the description of the data
structure in order to
describe the "data-model"
(static aspect).
. EAR-analysis, information
analysis.

4.1.
<u>Data</u> structure = the ordered structure of mutu-
ally related data as manifest
in a process.
This ordering and the distin-
guishing of relations can be
performed in many ways as described in the litterature.

<u>a</u>. logical data structure, data
structure, (sub) schema, conceptual schema, objectschema,
informationbasis, object-
attribute-matrix, infological
model.

4.2.
<u>Data</u> - a logical element or group of
elements that can be distin-
guished and that has relevance
and semantic value. (see H.
Wedekind, (4).

<u>a</u>. "(structured) datum", object
(group), entity.
<u>b</u>. client, product.

<u>4.3.</u>
<u>Data</u> element = a component that forms together with other components a data (datum). Data elements can belong to several data.

  <u>a</u>. "datum element", property (type), attribute, feature, variable.
  <u>b</u>. clientnumber, producttype.

<u>4.4.</u>
<u>Element</u> type = the specification of a data element by a defined name, a defined symbol.
An element type is defined by a name and a range (value area).

  <u>a</u>. data type
  <u>b</u>. CNR (100-999), PRT (A-F).

  N.B. The fact that data elements can belong to several data makes the description of the final datastructure an almost impossible task. In most cases it is tried to show this structure in data-diagramms, see for example:
  . Wedekind - schema for an ob
                 jectgroup
  . Codasyl - schema, subschema
  . Nijssen - conceptual schema,
                 external schema.

<u>4.5.</u>
<u>Data</u> relation = the mutually interwoven data caused by the fact that data elements can belong to several data. The relations can be shown in the form of a table (matrix), a graph/schema or a 'list'.

  <u>a</u>. relationship (in EAR), objectrelation, entity role (see Swanson).

4.6.

Information   = the physical signals that are, through a sensorial observation/perception, submitted to a syntactic ordening (data element) and to a semantic meaning/signification (message) and to a relevance in order to contribute to the knowledge of one or more humans.

4.7.

Message,   = an ordered series of data elements with a semantic meaning.
Information flow
N.B. See H. Wedekind, E.B. Swanson, C.J. Date, Starreveld.

The following figure is from Wedekind's "System analyse":

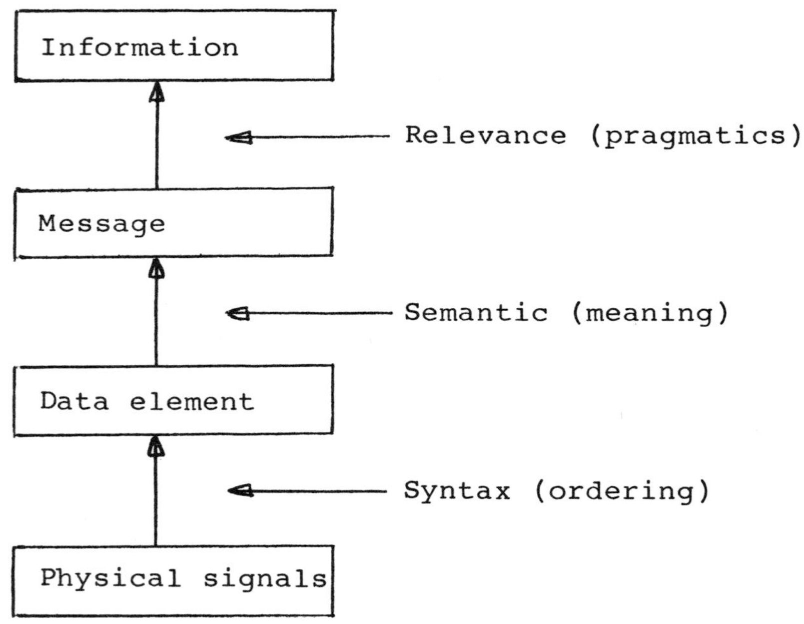

5.

Project   = the execution of a number of activities, actions with the aim to reach a goal that has been specified before, the furnishing of a 'product' described beforehand.

For this the needed means (manpower, money and tools) are supplied, whereby the execution of these activities is limited in time by a begin and end date

<u>a</u> "a project-wise approach stimulates the process-intrinsic motivation possibilities of the personnel".

<u>b</u> the design of a CAD-system for the development of car-prototypes. (N.B. Once designed and in use this system belongs to the whole car-production-process).

5.1

Project phasing = the grouping of projectactivities into project phases, that can be executed either in parallel or in sequence/order of succession.

<u>a</u> project steps
<u>b</u> feasibility study, logical design, etc.

N.B. In most cases this phasing aims at the control of the project execution in such a way that the results of each phase can be well defined.

5.2

Project planning= the planning of the activities to be executed in time together with the estimation of elapse time and manpower needed both quantatively as well as qualitatively per phase.

5.3.
**Project
activity**
= the description of an action to be executed for a particular project phase.

<u>b</u> the interview of a person, the preparation of a report.

5.4.
**Project
organisation**
= the organisation of the personnel needed for the project execution.

N.B. In most cases an organisation with steering group and project groups is suggested. The project personnel is recruited generally on a part-time basis from the company for the duration of the project. The steering group mostly gets the mandate from the company management for that period.

<u>a</u> matrix organisation.

5.5.
**Project
management**
= the responsibility for the day-to-day affairs is mostly bestowed upon a temporary projectmanager/projectleader.

5.6.
**Project
secretary**
= the group of people in charge of the execution of the administrative duties for the project

5.7.
**Project
documentation**
= the documentation of all the results created during project execution, for example reports, documentation of the feasibility study, system documentation, program documentation, documentation on behalf of projectmanagement.

Appendix 3

Comparison of terminology.

In the following table, a comparison of the terms as used in the ten methods is given. As a frame of reference, the terms and definitions as given in appendix 2 have been used. In most cases, the meaning of a term used in one of the ten methodologies is not strictly comparable to any of the terms as given in appendix 2. Three cases can be distinguished:
-the meaning does exactly coincide

notation: A=B　　*
-the meaning of the term in the methodology is contained in the meaning of the term in the appendix and is "narrower"

notation: A　B
-the meaning of the term in the methodology covers (fully or partially) the meaning of the term in the appendix, but is "broader"

notation: A　B

Additionally to this comparison, per methodology some of the most characteristic terms are mentioned.

*　"A" refers to the term in appendix 2, "B" refers to the term in the methodology

Terms	I BSP	II SADT
1. Process		
1.1 Sub (sub)process		1.1=administrative structure
		1.1⊃system
1.2 Elementary process	1.2=Key process	
1.3 Activity	1.3=activity	1.3=activity
1.4 Process function		
1.5 Process flow		1.5=functional specification
2. Corporate analysis/synthesis		
2.1 Process relations	2.1=process relations	2.1⊂relationships
2.2 Corporate model	2.2⊃information system plan	2.2⊃requirements specs
(dyn.)	2.2⊃company processes	2.2⊃operational requirements
(dyn.)	2.2⊃network of information systems	
(dyn.)	2.2⊃management control process	
	2.2⊃operations proces	
	2.2⊃information architecture	
3. Process analysis (dynamic aspect)		
3.1 Information system (IS)	3.1=information system	3.1⊃viewpoint
3.2 Information sub (sub) system		3.1=SA-activities model
3.3 Elementary inf. system		(dyn.)
3.4 Process model	3.4⊂network of inform.syst.	3.4 system archit.
	3.4⊂generic info. syst.network	-operational
		-technical
		-economical
3.5 IS-data relation		3.5 SA data model
4. Data analysis (static aspect)		
		(dyn.)
		(dyn.)
4.1 Data structure		4.1=SA-data model
4.2 Data		
4.3 Data element		4.3=data
4.4 Elementtype	4.4⊂data classes	
4.5 Datarelation		4.5⊂relationships

III ISAC	IV MOS	V SASO
1.0=activity		
	1.2=elementary process	1.2=elementary process
1.5)data system design	1.5)operational procedure description	1.5)user procedures
	2.1)process flow schema	
(dyn.) 2.2)logical systemstruct.		2.2)objectsystem 2.2)objectsystem analysis
3.0)activity analysis 3.0)process analysis 3.1=information system	3.0)information analysis 3.0)activity analysis 3.1)technical systemstruct.	3.1=information system
3.3)program design 3.3(data structure design and pro- gram boundary determination 3.4=system hierarchy 3.4)system relations		3.3=independent procedure 3.4)determination of system boundary
4.0(precedence analysis 4.0=component analysis 4.1(information schema 4.1(data structure design and program boun- dary determ.	4.0)component analysis 4.0)data analysis 4.0)object analysis 4.1(conceptual data model	4.1)component analysis 4.1)data analysis
		4.5(coupling/ binding

Terms	I BSP	II SADT
4.6 Information		
4.7 Message, infor- mation flow	4.7⟩data class	
5. Project		

5.1 Projectphasing	5.1⟨corporate plan
	5.1⟨information
	  system plan
	5.1⟩bottom-up
	  implementation
	5.1=information
	  life cycle
		5.1⟩design
		  constraints

5.2 Projectplanning	5.2=action plan	
5.3 Projectactivity		5.3⟩walk-through 5.3⟩review
5.4 Project- organisation	5.4⟩Projectteam	5.4=SADT project- team

5.5 Project-
management
	5.5 information
	  systems
	  management
	5.5⟩BSP study
	  control file
		5.5⟩technical
		  management
		5.5⟩projectmanager

5.6 Project secretary		5.6⟩project libra- rian

5.7 Project-
documentation
	5.7⟩four quadrant
	  matrix
	5.7⟩interview
	  analysis and
	  data reduction
	  sheet
		5.7=SADT-diagrams
		5.7=structured
		  analysis-
		  language

	I BSP Additional	II SADT Additional

	- organisation
	  units
	- top-down
	  analysis
	- corporate prio-
	  rities
	- bottom up
	  implementation
	- business process
	  matrix
	- organisation
	  process matrix
	- system process
	  matrix
	- problem process
	  matrix
	- prerequisite sub-
	  system analysis
	  matrix
	- input process-
	  output diagram
		- author, commen-
		  tor, chiefana-
		  list, instructor,
		  readers, experts,
		  technical commit-
		  tee
		- SADT-constraints
		- system require-
		  ments
		- economical cost/
		  benefit aspects
		- administrative
		  structure
		- walk through
		- review
		- configuration
		  management
		- top-down analysis
		- structured
		  analysis-language
		- constraints
		- things=data
		- desk checking

III ISAC	IV MOS	V SASO
4.6=information 4.7⊂system relation	4.7=elementary info-sets	4.7=elementary info-sets 4.7=dialogue design
5.1⊃information analysis 5.1⊂choice of change- approach		
5.4=project- organisation		
5.7⊃A,C,D,P,I graphs	5.7⊃precedence schemes, I-set	
Additional - success of info.syst. - change analysis - top-down ana- lysis - choice of change approach - interest groups - problem groups tabel - table of objectives - property tabel - equipment study - precedence- analysis	Additional - top-down decom- position - precedence analysis - change analysis - entity relations model - coupling and binding rules - incedence matrix - process flow schema - dataset process matrix	Additional - objectives analysis - systemboundary determination - precedence analysis - top-down - normalisation (Date) - coupling and binding

Terms	VI NIAM	VII BUBBLE-CHARTING
1. <u>Process</u>		
1.1 Sub (sub)process	1.1=conceptual transaction	
1.2 Elementary process		
1.3 Activity		
1.4 Process function	1.4=process	
1.5 Process flow		
2. <u>Corporate analysis/synthesis</u>		
2.1 <u>Process relations</u>	2.1⊂process analysis	
2.2 Corporate model		
3. <u>Process analysis (dynamic aspect)</u>		
3.1 Information system (IS)	3.1=(administrative) information system	
3.2 Information sub (sub) system		
3.3 Elementary inf. system		
3.4 Process model	3.4=information flowdiagram	
3.5 IS-data relation	3.5⊃derived sentences 3.5 information analysis	
4. <u>Data analysis (static aspect)</u>	4.0⊂information analysis	
4.1 Data structure	4.1=conceptual schema 4.1⊂DD/D 4.1⊂coexistence architecture 4.1⊃presciptive grammar 4.1⊃internal, external schema	4.1⊃canonical data-structures 4.1⊃logical datamodel
4.2 Data		
4.3 Data element		4.3⊃main key 4.3⊃identifier 4.3⊃attribute 4.3⊃primary key 4.3⊃secundary key

VIII WARNIER/ORR	IX JACKSON	X PSL/PSA
		1.1=process
1.2=function	1.2=action	1.2=process
		1.3=process
	1.4=synchronisation process	1.4=processor
	1.4 function	
	1.5)state vector	1.5=event,condition,
	1.5)data stream	trigger
	2.1)life history	2.1(synthetic and
	2.1)entity structure	analytical
	2.1 system specification diagram	relationships
	2.1 system timing diagram	
		2.2)event,condition, trigger
		3.1 target system
3.2)function-analysis		
3.3=function model		
	3.4)program structure diagram	
	3.4)program structure text	
	3.5)datastructure diagram	
4.1)hierarchical DB design	4.1(initial model	
4.1)(logical) data-base		
4.2='derived'item		4.2)relation, data
		4.2(set, entity group
		4.3=group, element

Terms	VI NIAM	VII BUBBLE-CHARTING
4.4 Elementtype	4.4(objects	

4.5 Datarelation	4.5=role
	4.5 elementary
	    sentence
	4.5) semantic of
	    sentences
	4.5 relation type
		4.5) functional
		    dependency

4.6 Information		

4.7 Message, infor-
    mation flow
	4.7) elementary
	    sentence
	4.7) trigger
	4.7=logical unit of
	    information
		4.7=information
		    requirement

5. Project 5.1 Projectphasing 5.2 Projectplanning 5.3 Projectactivity		

5.4 Project-
    organisation
5.5 Project-
    management
5.6 Project
    secretary
5.7 Project-
    documentation
		5.7) Bubble-Chart

	Additional
	- object-types
	- constraints
	  (screening
	  procedures)
	- roles
	- elementairy
	  sentence
	- meta information
	  base
	- source
	- sinks
	- (rules of) grammar
	- DD/D infobase
	  handler
	- prescriptive
	  grammar
	- conceptual schema
	- internal schema
	- storage schema
		Additional
		- normalisation

VIII WARNIER/ORR	IX JACKSON	X PSL/PSA
		4.4(PSL/PSA attribute state-ments
4.5)logical operators	4.5(data structure diagram	4.5(synthetical and analytical relation ships
		4.5)object types, objects
	4.6 entity	4.6)object statements
4.7=desired output	4.7=data structure	4.7=input, output
	4.7=input,output data	4.7)aspect
	4.7(state vector	4.7(interface
5.7)Warnier-diagram	5.7)structure diagram	5.7(automated documentation system
Additional	Additional	Additional
- structured programming	- entity	- input parameters
- sequention	- action	- output parameters
- repetition	- life history	- meta data
- selection	- entity/action step	- commands
- logical update actions	- entity structure step	- attribute
- to achieve the goal by iteration	- initial model step	- system aspects:
- precedence analysis	- function step	- data oriented
	- system timing step	- process oriented
	- implementation step	- relationship oriented
	- time grain marker	- system dynamics oriented
	- synchronization process	- object types
	- program inversion	
	- program dismembering	
	- pseudo-code